Greetings from Alabama

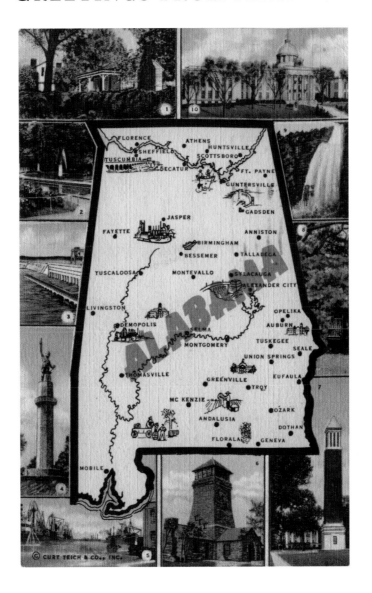

The main street of Alabama's capital city, early 1900s.

GREETINGS FROM ALABAMA

A Pictorial History in Vintage Postcards

FROM THE WADE HALL COLLECTION
OF HISTORICAL PICTURE POSTCARDS
FROM ALABAMA

WADE H. HALL

WITH NANCY B. DuPREE
AND CHRISTOPHER SAWULA

NewSouth Books

Montgomery

NewSouth Books
105 S. Court Street
Montgomery, AL 36104

Copyright © 2016.
All rights reserved under International and Pan-American Copyright Conventions. Published in the
United States by NewSouth Books, a division of NewSouth, Inc., Montgomery, Alabama.

Publisher's Cataloging-in-Publication Data

Hall, Wade H.
Greetings from Alabama : a pictorial history in vintage postcards :
from the Wade Hall collection of historical picture postcards from Alabama /
Wade H. Hall with Nancy B. DuPree and Christopher Sawula
p. cm

ISBN 978-1-58838-320-4 (paperback)

1. Alabama—History—Pictorial works. 2. Postcards—Alabama. I. Title.

2016949671

Design by Randall Williams

Printed in South Korea through
Four Colour Print Group, Louisville, Kentucky

Contents

Dr. Wade Hall, circa 1990, on one of his "collecting" trips during which he scoured flea markets, garage sales, and antique outlets for postcards of Alabama and Kentucky.

Foreword

LOUIS A. PITSCHMANN

Greetings from Alabama is a representative sampling of the much larger Wade Hall Postcard Collection at Troy University Library, Troy, Alabama. Dr. Hall began acquiring postcards in the late 1970s and continued to collect for more than thirty years. His interest in historical postcards stemmed from knowing a group of deltiologists, or as he enjoyed saying, "a fancy word for one who collects and studies postcards." The Hall Collection today comprises some 25,000 postcards depicting scenes from all fifty states; approximately 2,000 of these depict Alabama locations.

Unlike other collectors whose focus may be a specific era in postcard production, a specific printer, or theme—such as cards depicting railroad stations or trains—Dr. Hall's interest in postcards lay in how they depicted a particular place, its business districts, residential streets, architecture, commerce, or simply its landscape. He once described his motivation to collect as a desire "to document in words and pictures the culture that had shaped me and was beginning to fade as people adjusted to the new ways and inventions of the 20th century." With this as his primary motivation, combined with his strong sense of identity with his home state, he made postcards depicting scenes from Alabama a major collecting focus. Over time, what he assembled evolved into an important research collection for anyone interested in the pictorial history of Alabama from the late nineteenth to the mid-twentieth century. Researchers and collectors alike will find that the Collection documents long-lost railroad stations, schools, businesses, even churches and synagogues, many of which with the passage of time fell victim to the whims of Mother Nature (tornadoes, fires, floods) or the whims of man (urban renewal projects, interstate highway development). Many of the rural scenes depicted in his collection are today merely "pictures on a postcard" having fallen victim to the ravages of time itself: the gradual deterioration of structures exposed to the elements or the loss of once-fertile fields now overtaken by real estate developments or overgrown by kudzu and scrub pines after Alabama's rural economy moved from cotton to catfish farms and natural resources.

In the late 1990s, Dr. Hall came to believe his

collection should be placed in an academic setting where it could be preserved and its ongoing availability could be ensured as a teaching tool and a resource for scholars studying the history of Alabama's architecture and economic development. Troy University, where he had earned his bachelor's degree some fifty years earlier, proved to be an ideal location. Shortly after placing the Collection there in 2001, he approached the University of Alabama Libraries with the proposal that the University Libraries partner with Troy University Library to digitize the Alabama portion. That project led to the creation of nearly 4,000 digital images capturing both the front and the back of each card so that not only the scene was preserved but also the name of the addressee and the message.

His desire to digitize the Alabama postcards was only one part of a larger plan to promote use of the Collection. For several years prior to his passing in 2015, he had hoped to publish in book form a broad sample of his Alabama postcards in an effort to reach an even wider audience, as he had already done in 1994 with his historical postcards of Kentucky. Numerous other interests and obligations unfortunately prevented him from realizing that plan. Bringing his concept to reality was ultimately left to others with whom he had discussed his hopes.

Determining the most representative cards to include, their organization, and description became a team-effort commitment to realizing Dr. Hall's plan. In particular, I wish to acknowledge Suzanne La Rosa and Randall Williams of NewSouth

Books for the support and enthusiasm with which they embraced this project. Mr. Williams also gave generously of his knowledge of publishing and book design by advising on the organization of content. His colleague, editorial assistant Brandie Johnson, made the final selection of some 400 postcards and arranged them geographically within the book. The earlier Herculean task of winnowing thousands of images to a manageable preliminary selection of some 900, and preparing captions for those which appear in this book, was deftly carried out by Dr. Nancy B. DuPree and Dr. Christopher Sawula in the Division of Special Collections at the University of Alabama Libraries. Without Dr. DuPree's extensive knowledge of Alabama's political, economic, and social history and Dr. Sawula's prior experience with public history projects, this publication would simply not have been feasible.

Troy University Library has been equally enthusiastic in seeing *Greetings from Alabama* become a reality. Lastly, it should not go unstated that this publication owes much to a generous monetary gift Dr. Hall made to the University of Alabama Libraries in 2009 explicitly to promote the use of his various collections now housed in the Division of Special Collections at the University of Alabama.

Louis A. Pitschmann, PhD, Dean of Libraries, the University of Alabama, 2001–2015.

VIII

Editor's Note

As noted earlier by Dean Louis Pitschmann, Wade Hall long intended to publish an Alabama companion to his 1994 University of Kentucky Press volume, *Greetings from Kentucky: A Post Card Tour, 1900–1950*. In fact, he dropped off a copy of the Kentucky book during a trip back to Alabama soon after its release; the inscription is dated Christmas '94. At the time, he was still living and teaching in Louisville, but his mind and his heart were never far from his home state, and we were just beginning to work with him on what became *Conecuh People: Words of Life from the Alabama Black Belt*, a combination oral history and memoir of his roots in Bullock County.

Conecuh People finally appeared in 1998, but it was another decade before Wade, his partner, Gregg Swem, and their massive collections of books, art, photographs, quilts, letters, and other collectibles moved back to Hall's Crossroads south of Union Springs. Among all those boxes and file cabinets were the 2,000 Alabama-themed postcards that have ended up at Troy University and the University of Alabama.

Throughout the last twenty years of Wade's life, few conversations with him about any editorial matters concluded without at least a passing reference to his "Alabama postcard book." The Kentucky book was to be a model, though his notions for organization of the Alabama volume were different.

Wade was, however, a man of many interests and abilities, and between the publication of *Greetings from Kentucky* and his death in 2015, he wrote and published plays, musicals, biographies, local histories, and poems, oversaw the making of *Conecuh People* into an acclaimed play and tourist attraction, established and endowed a literary award and lecture series, and supervised the dissemination of his collection among a half-dozen institutions. And grew tomatoes and built a fish pond.

Greetings from Alabama, meanwhile, never got beyond the outline and discussion stage, but after his passing, the University of Alabama Libraries commissioned its completion. The present volume is the result of Wade's years of collecting and is faithful to his vision. The essay that follows, under his byline, is adapted posthumously from his introduction to the Kentucky book, with additions based on his notes and comments over the years. I believe he would like it.

— HORACE RANDALL WILLIAMS

Heidelberg, Germany.

Wade Hall, U.S. Army, Heidelberg, Germany.

Introduction

WADE H. HALL

I don't remember the first time I ever *received* a picture postcard, but the first time I ever sent one was from Heidelberg, Germany, in the mid-1950s, when I was in the U.S. Army. I had just arrived from the States, and I wanted my family to *see* what Germany looked like. I went to the Post Exchange and selected a bird's-eye view of the city taken from the top of a nearby mountain. In the weeks and months that followed, I mailed dozens of picture postcards back home to friends and relatives. I was able to show my distant readers, none of whom had ever been to Europe, what I was seeing as I traveled around Germany, France, Switzerland, Austria, Belgium, Luxembourg, Holland, and England. It was a pattern of communication that had been set in the United States as early as 1893 with postcard views of the World's Columbian Exposition in Chicago as the nation celebrated the four hundredth anniversary of the European discovery of the New World.

Like wildfire, the postcard fad spread and before the turn of the new century, many towns and cities throughout the nation had their main streets, churches and schools, scenic views and monuments, and famous citizens depicted on postcards. They were not only inexpensive and convenient but beautiful forms of democratic art that anyone could afford. Soon people began to form postcard clubs, collecting cards from all over the country, and placing them carefully in attractive albums that enjoyed a place of honor in middle-class parlors next to the family Bible. This buying and sending and collecting craze continued until after World War I, when their popularity abated somewhat as the nation's tastes in popular art became more sophisticated and other forms of personal communication began to compete. Moreover, the artistic quality of the postcard images had declined because the trade in cards produced by skilled German printers had been stopped by the war.

Nevertheless, the picture postcard had become a fixture in American life. Even as recently as the end of the twentieth century, despite the omnipresence of the telephone and the fax machine (but tellingly before near universal use of Facebook, Instagram, Snapchat, etc.), few people left home for more than a couple of days without mailing back postcard views and comments on their trip. Postcards were still a handy and effective way of saying, "Arrived safely. Here is where I am. Wish you were here." This colorful record had a dimension lacking in a letter or the plain vanilla government postal card. Indeed, beginning in the 1970s there was a resurgence of interest in collecting vintage as well as contemporary cards. Thousands of people belonged again to postcard clubs and tens of thousands attended postcard shows each year. Such people are called deltiologists, a fancy word for one who sends, receives, collects, and studies postcards.

Although there is a great deal of overlapping, deltiologists usually divide postcard history into seven periods. The Pioneer Period stemmed from "Private Mailing Cards" that carried a mailing rate reduced from two cents to one cent, the same as the government-issue cards, which had been available since 1873. It was also in 1898 that the mailing of postcards received another boost when Congress authorized Rural Free Delivery, which made sending and receiving all types of mail easy and inexpensive for the majority of Americans who still lived in rural areas. "Mail riders," as country people often called them, made front-yard deliveries and pick-ups on horseback and buggy and later by automobile.

This Private Mailing Card Period (1898–1901) began the mania for postcard sending and collecting. Postcard clubs and publications sprouted all over the land. The Undivided Back Period (1901–07) permitted only "Post Card" to be printed on the address side. No personal message was allowed, except whatever the sender could squeeze in on or around the picture. The Divided Back Period (1907–15) allowed a personal greeting on the left side of a vertical line, with the address on the right side. By then, hardly anyone left home without promising to mail back a chain of cards that chronicled the traveler's journey. Cards were readily available almost anywhere, in such places as train stations, drugstores, hotels, book and stationary shops, and souvenir stands and could be

Above, examples of cards from the "Undivided Back" and "Divided Back" periods, respectively; opposite page, from top, examples of the "White Border," "Linen," and "Chrome" period cards, respectively.

19TH STREET LOOKING NORTH FROM 1ST AVENUE, BIRMINGHAM, ALA.

KELLER MEMORIAL BRIDGE, DECATUR, ALA.

mailed at convenient mail drops and even on board trains at Railroad Post Offices.

The White Border Period (1916–30) was ushered in by the world war, when almost all postcards were produced by domestic manufacturers. They were printed with white borders that were supposed to save ink. For many collectors this period signaled the end of collectible postcards. The sixth or Linen Period (1930–45) produced cards on textured paper, often using garish inks that sometimes faded. Cards during this period were frequently based on black and white photographs that had been reworked by artists, then painted in watercolors before printing. The process produced an often stylized, surreal image that collectors are now beginning to value. Postcards of the final or Chrome Period (since 1945) are usually glossy color copies of color photographs. During this period advances in color photography have made it possible to produce cards with sharp, color-correct images made from transparencies, or, more recently, digitally.

All periods of postcards are now collected and treasured for their artistic and historical values, but most collectors are still partial to those that portray eras rapidly vanishing from human memory.

Collectors are also increasingly intrigued by the messages that these cards carried. Because of the cramped writing space, especially before 1907, there developed

This portrait of Wade Hall's ancestors in Bullock County, Alabama, is typical of the subject matter captured in the "Real Photo" postcards that became popular in the early 1900s.

XIV

a postcard shorthand made up of inventive abbreviations: "Arr OK. Saw bro Seth at rr stat. Go to ss and ch Sun." Collectors are also attracted by photograph cards, or Real Photos, made possible in 1902 when the Eastman Kodak Company introduced a camera and postcard-size paper on which photographs could be printed directly from negatives. This invention made it possible for almost anyone to have personalized cards featuring his or her own likeness.

From the beginning, of course, postcard subjects reflected the broad tastes and interests of the American people, from comic cards with ethnic barbs directed at the Irish or Scots or Indians or blacks or hillbillies to those that celebrated religious holidays and holy images. Postcards

were designed for every special day on the calendar from New Year's Day to St. Patrick's Day to Halloween to Groundhog Day. It has been estimated that as many as 10,000 different Santa Claus cards have been issued. There were also brightly embossed cards designed by such talented artists as Ellen Clapsaddle, Frances Brundage, and H. B. Griggs. Such special events as fairs, chautauquas, political conventions, and expositions were promoted. Famous people, historical and contemporary, were honored with cards. There were novelty cards that talked, sang, or popped up or were decorated with ribbons, real hair, and dried flowers. Women with common names such as Martha or Sarah or Adelaide could buy cards with their names embossed on them. Current events produced many cards, often with a satirical bent. The Woman's Suffrage Movement, for example, was a popular target. A 1910 card shows a henpecked husband dressed in a maid's apron on his knees cleaning the floor, saying plaintively, "My wife's joined the Suffrage Movement (I've suffered ever since!)."

In addition, all-purpose generic cards could be used to represent any place. A circa 1909 card showing a smartly dressed woman detraining with hordes of people welcoming her, reads: "They gave me a great reception at _____." The purchaser could fill in the blank with her destination. A bevy of beautiful girls could serve as "the Girls of Birmingham" or "the Girls of Dothan." Other generic cards showed identical rural scenes and could be inscribed variously. Among this huge variety, however, it was the view card showing actual places that dominated the industry from the start. Cards showing main streets (like "Washington Street looking east, Demopolis, Ala."), important buildings, hotels, restaurants, and tourist attractions could show the folks at home what you were seeing. View cards of Alabama became instant bestsellers with Alabamians as well as visitors. State pride created ready turf for the introduction of postcards featuring Alabama images. Although some cards printed before 1900 are extant, it was not until early in the twentieth century that travelers could find views of just about any place in the state, from Fairfax to Fort Payne, from Brundidge to Bessemer. In October of 1906, Dave in Mobile sent Miss Matt Shadburne in St. Matthews, Kentucky, a color photographic view of the "Toll Gate on Bay Shell Road" and exclaimed: "Hello Matt, In this city I hang my hat and call it home sweet home."

Bird's-eye cards of Alabama cities and towns showed high-view vistas of cityscapes. Close-up views of streets were also very popular, and through the years they show not only the architectural changes in homes and commercial buildings but also the evolution of transportation,

from wagons, buggies, and carriages to bicycles, trolleys, streetcars, and finally automobiles and buses. Moreover, postcards chronicle the wider progress of transportation in Alabama from steamboats to the air age. The coming of the affordable automobile in the 1900s gave a burst of popularity to postcards. Motorists could travel at their own convenience from place to place within the state and from Alabama to other states. They could stay at the older hotels or choose the newer tourist homes and cottages and motels. Sometimes the traveler would put an X by a room or a cottage, explaining, "This is where we slept last night." Furthermore, postcards provide us with a visual history of Alabama's roadside architecture—an elephant-shaped gas station near Roanoke, a quaint motel south of Anniston, the Bottle store near Auburn, Wigwam Village No. 5 at Bessemer, and numerous bridges spanning Alabama's waterways.

Postcards featuring such public places as

xv

Bay Shell Road, Mobile.

U. S. NATIONAL GUARD, CAMP SHERIDAN, MONTGOMERY, ALA.

ARMY Y.M.C.A.

ONE OF THE Y. M. C. A. BUILDINGS.

Where F. Scott Fitzgerald was stationed when he met Miss Zelda Sayre during World War I.

courthouses, churches, post offices, train depots, fire stations—even cemeteries and penal institutions—became very popular. Cards often provide us with documentation of buildings and institutions that no longer exist. Where are Alabama Synodical College for Women in Talladega, Central Female College in Tuscaloosa, the second Jewett Hall at Judson College, the Lanett Bleachery and Dye Works in what is now called Valley, or the magnificent Robert Taylor-designed chapel that used to stand on the Tuskegee Institute campus? They are all gone with the years, but on postcards they left images as bright as today.

Even some activities and situations that give us pause today are celebrated on Alabama's postcards. Moonshine stills graced many a card sent from Alabama around the globe and unfortunately helped perpetuate the state's image as a backward, scofflaw state. Our image abroad probably was also not enhanced by messages like this one on the back of a black and white print of Dexter Avenue, the state capital's main street, sent in February 1906 to Norwood in Cheshire, England: "This is a Fine city in Alabama—Everybody carries a gun in his pocket & they always have one behind the counter in the saloons. Kou."

There is nothing like a grand tragedy to bring out the cameras and, quickly following, postcard views that have commemorated Alabama's natural and manmade disasters: a devastating flood in Elba, a powerful hurricane in Mobile, an automobile accident. Brave firefighters and selfless soldiers are depicted on many cards as heroes in time of distress. Alabama's role in our nation's wars is reflected on cards of soldiers and scenes at Fort Rucker, Fort McClelland, Moton Field, and Camp Sheridan, stretching, on historical cards, all the way back to the Civil War. Real Photo cards allowed young men to pretend that they were wild and wooly cowboys playing in a saloon—all within the safe walls of a photographer's studio in Montgomery or Birmingham. Other Real Photo cards show individuals and families in exotic studio settings or in front of their homes and barns, sometimes with a new wagon and horse in the foreground.

Real and imagined historic sites have been favorites with Alabamians and visitors alike: the Indian mounds at Moundville; the abandoned columns of a once-great house at Cahaba; the advertising-covered barn-hangar of the Wright Brothers' short-lived flying school in Montgomery, the vistas overlooking the site of the Battle of Horseshoe Bend in Tallapoosa County, and Helen Keller's home in Tuscumbia. Also featured on numerous postcards are the homes of such state luminaries as author Augusta Evans Wilson of Mobile, educator Booker T. Washington in Tuskegee, and Coca-Cola bottler Walter Bellingrath in

Mobile County, and, more recently, Hank Williams in Greenville.

Alabama's rich religious heritage is reflected on cards showing the First Presbyterian Church in Anniston; St. John's Episcopal in Montgomery, where Jefferson Davis rented a pew; and the "colored" First Baptist Church in Montgomery, where the National Baptist Convention was organized. Needless to say, there are many postcard views of

Atop Alabama's highest peak, Mt. Cheaha.

local Baptist, Methodist, Presbyterian, Catholic, Jewish, and Episcopal churches from across the state.

Politics, a major Alabama occupation and pre-occupation, is documented on postcards featuring photographs of the officeholders themselves or of statues erected in their honor. In 1911, fifty years after the Civil War, ceremonies and dedications of memorials were popular postcard subjects. Of course, the Confederacy easily won the monument war, with dozens of postcards depicting public statues honoring the fallen heroes of the Lost Cause.

Famous Alabama natives or adoptees graced many a postcard, from Helen Keller to Emma Sansom, from Admiral Raphael Semmes to football hero turned actor Johnny Mack Brown. Sadly, racism explains the rarity of cards featuring significant Alabamians like Nat King Cole, W. C. Handy, Jesse Owens, and Joe Louis.

Other popular genres of Alabama postcards included resorts, sports and sports venues, commercial establishments and products, restaurants and hotels, and scenic views of nature, from the Gulf Coast to Mount Cheaha.

The documentary photographer Walker Evans once wrote in *Fortune* magazine that postcards are "some of the truest visual records ever made of any period." That assertion, however, is an inflated claim, and a word of caution is in order when using postcard images or printed statements as documentary evidence. Postcards usually tell the truth, but they can also tell half-truths and occasionally lies. Postcard images, for example, may be carefully contrived and manipulated to present a preconceived view of a person or a place or an issue. Business owners who wanted their shops or tourist cabins or eateries spruced up by the printer's artist would have them apply a new coat of paint or remove an unsightly building or tree or place a new convertible at the curb of a drive-in restaurant. Furthermore, suppositions and theories are sometimes given as facts.

Nonetheless, in these pages you will see the panorama that was Alabama for the first half of the twentieth century. This is, indeed, the way we were—from a view of Tuscumbia's Main Street in 1907 to a drive-in restaurant near Auburn in 1950.

Travel Alabama from top to bottom. Look and enjoy.

GREETINGS FROM ALABAMA

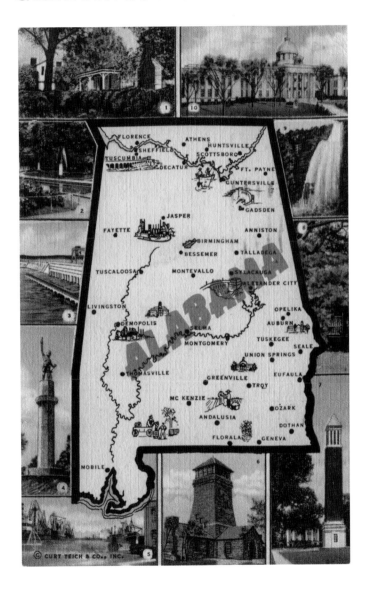

Alabama Counties

⪦ A NOTE ON ORGANIZATION ⪧

The postcards that follow are loosely arranged by county, from the southwest corner of the state to the northeast, winding from west to east and back to west then back to east and so forth across and up the state from south to north. Larger counties like Mobile, Montgomery, Jefferson, Madison, and Tuscaloosa have individual sections and headlines; smaller counties are grouped with their neighbors under regional headings. The county depicted in the postcards on a particular page is indicated by the shaded area on the small state outline above the page number.

MOBILE COUNTY

A TYPICAL SOUTHERN SUNSET OVER THE BAY, MOBILE, ALA.

Mobile Bay, the fourth largest estuary in the U.S., was first settled by Native Americans attracted by its abundant resources. Its lush beauty has attracted tourists ever since, including French, Spanish, and British colonists and free and enslaved Africans.

TURNER TERMINALS, MOBILE, ALA.—3

TURNER TERMINAL COMPANY.

Turner Terminal Co., founded by Horace Turner, built facilities in the Port of Mobile to transfer freight between ships and trains, boosting commerce between New York and Mobile.

Begun in 1703, Mobile's Mardi Gras is the oldest Carnival celebration in the U.S., and its Cowbellion de Rakin Society, founded in 1830, was the first American mystic society. The group expanded to New Orleans in 1835.

4

Dauphin Street was the center of Mobile's historic commercial district. Many of the buildings still stand. The Gayfer's sign in the center marked the store begun in 1879 by C. J. Gayfer, noted for new ideas such as worker health care.

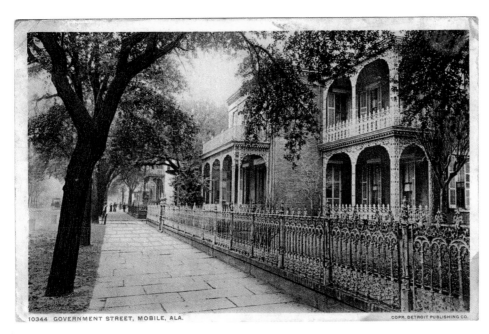

10344 GOVERNMENT STREET, MOBILE, ALA.   COPR. DETROIT PUBLISHING CO.

During the late 19th and early 20th centuries, Government Street was known for its mansions and large estates. The ornamental ironwork—"iron lace"—appeared in many forms, including the ornate examples shown here. Many mansions were replaced by office buildings.

10345. OLD MARKET HOUSE, MOBILE, ALA.

Mrs. John Craft

Mobile's Old Market and City Hall was completed in 1857. Modified several times over the years and damaged in a 1979 hurricane, the Italianate-style complex of buildings was restored in 1997 to house the History Museum of Mobile. The structure is a National Historic Landmark.

5

The first Battle House Hotel burned in 1905. The second was built in 1908 to a design by Frank M. Andrews of New York City. President Woodrow Wilson was a guest in 1913. The hotel closed in 1974 but was restored in 2007. It now operates as the Battle House Renaissance Mobile Hotel.

BATTLE HOUSE, MOBILE, ALABAMA.

6

Now known as Ladd-Peebles Stadium, the celebrated football arena was privately funded in 1948 by a local banker as a memorial to his mentor, Ernest F. Ladd. The first game, between Alabama and Vanderbilt, ended in a 14–14 tie. The annual Senior Bowl has been played here since 1951.

BIENVILLE SQUARE, MOBILE, ALA.—102

Bienville Square takes up an entire city block and has been a park since the land was given to Mobile by the United States Congress in 1824. The Square is home to many Mobile functions and hosted a 1905 speech by President Theodore Roosevelt.

7

CAWTHON HOTEL, MOBILE, ALA.—98

AZALEA TIME IN MOBILE

The Cawthon Hotel was built in 1907 on Bienville Square. By the 1950s, it was advertised as "Fireproof," "Completely Air-Cooled," and just "3 short blocks from Bankhead Tunnel on U.S. Highway 90."

Mobile, Ala.   5178 Trinity Episcopal Church

MANUFACTURED BY CURT TEICH & CO., CHICAGO, ILL.

Trinity Episcopal Church, designed by architects Frank Wills and Henry Dudley, was the first Gothic Revival church in Alabama. Begun in 1845, it was not completed until 1857 due to delays caused by a yellow fever epidemic. The structure was added to the National Register of Historic Places in 1990.

Spain and France and England and the Old South, grown harmonious through the mellowing of time, are echoes in the streets.

— CARL CARMER, *Stars Fell on Alabama*, 1934

CONVENT OF VISITATION. MOBILE, ALA.

The Romanesque Revival-style Sacred Heart Chapel, center, was built in 1895. Operated as a women's academy by the Convent of the Visitation, it included a grammar and a high school. The school was closed by 1952 and restored from 1985–91 to serve as a retreat house.

Father Ryan's Monument, Mobile, Ala.

Father Abram Ryan (1838–86) was a Catholic priest, Confederate chaplain, and a popular poet of the Southern cause. The last verse of his most famous poem, "The Conquered Banner," is inscribed on his monument, which was erected in Father Ryan Park on North Bayou Street after a 1913 public fundraising drive.

9

Irish Catholic Patrick J. Lyons worked his way up from riverboat deckhand to become a wealthy businessman and politician in Mobile from about 1880 to 1920. A leader in the Progressive Era, he promoted waterworks, recreation, and other public goods, like this park eventually named in his honor.

10

The bronze statue of Confederate Admiral Raphael Semmes, erected in 1900, overlooks the entrance to the Bankhead Tunnel in downtown Mobile. Semmes had commanded the raider CSS Alabama, which sank or captured 65 enemy ships.

123   Soldiers And Sailors Memorial, Mobile, Alabama

The Soldiers and Sailors Memorial was erected in 1926 by the Mothers Army and Navy League, in memory of local men who died in World War I. The memorial is built of Alabama marble, with bronze plaques listing the names of 61 fallen soldiers.

MOBILE, Ala. Confederate Rest. Magnolia Cemetery.

3/26-07

Ira. C. Banta.

Magnolia Cemetery opened in 1836 and is still active. Its Confederate soldier statue was sculpted by Matthew J. Lawler and was unveiled by Raphael Semmes on April 27, 1874. The statue was shattered by lightning in 1931. The bust section was salvaged and installed elsewhere in the cemetery.

The Conde-Charlotte House, also known as the Kirkbride Home, is a historic house museum that dates to 1822, when its earliest portions served as a courthouse and city jail within the bastions of Fort Condé. The main section of the house was added after 1849.

Kirkbride Home, Mobile, Ala.

From statehood on, Mobile's economy was built on the cotton trade, funneling fiber from across Alabama to textile mills in the North and overseas. Wharves and warehouses proliferated, and by 1860 Mobile ranked third after New Orleans and New York in total exports.

STEAMER LOADING COTTON AT STATE DOCKS, MOBILE, ALA.—88

101

Chapel At Spring Hill College
Mobile, Alabama

St. Joseph's Chapel, completed in 1910, is one of six buildings that form the main quadrangle at Spring Hill College. The chapel is built of brick in Gothic Revival style. Along with the rest of the quadrangle buildings, it is listed on the National Register of Historic Places.

13

Air Depot Groups At Formal Inspection
Brookley Field, Mobile, Alabama

111

Brookley Army Air Field opened in 1938 and became the major World War II supply base for the southeastern U.S. and the Caribbean, as well as Mobile's largest employer of both civilians and wartime personnel. Thousands trained at Brookley and deployed around the world. The base closed in 1969.

MOBILE, Ala. New Home of Augusta Evans Wilson.

Writing under her maiden name, Augusta Evans Wilson was Alabama's bestselling author of the 19th century. A fierce Confederate and later Lost Cause propagandist, she lived in this house at 930 Government Street from 1894 until her death in 1909.

At risk of demolition in recent years, Barton Academy, circa 1839, was the state's first public school. The Greek Revival edifice on Government Street is named for legislator Willoughby Barton, who introduced the bill creating a school board—also the state's first—in Mobile in 1826.

14

Barton Academy.

The Bienville Hotel was on the north side of Bienville Square. When it opened in 1900, it advertised the latest conveniences, including a wash basin in each room and a bath for each two rooms. The roof garden offered live music and moving pictures. Lunch was 35 cents. It was torn down in the 1960s.

NEW UNION STATION, MOBILE, ALA.

Completed in 1907 for the old Mobile and Ohio Railroad, this terminal was designed by Architect P. Thorton Mayre and cost $575,000. It served passenger traffic until the 1950s and was used by the railroad until 1986. It was placed on the National Register in 1975. Since restored, it now houses offices.

15

The Episcopal Orphanage, also known as Wilmer Hall after founder Bishop Richard H. Wilmer, began in Tuscaloosa in 1864 and moved to Spring Hill in the early 1900s. The original campus of four Tudor-style cottages was expanded in 1968 and its mission was affirmed in 2008.

Episcopal Church Home, (Orphanage), Mobile, Ala.—25

16

Lushly landscaped Bellingrath Gardens encompasses 65 acres on the Fowl River outside Mobile. The estate was the home of Coca-Cola magnates Walter and Bessie Bellingrath until they opened it to the public in 1932. Now preserved by a foundation and recognized by state and federal historic registers, the site's floral displays attract thousands of visitors annually.

Bellingrath Gardens, Mobile, Alabama.

Interior Of Cathedral Of The Immaculate Conception, Mobile, Alabama 115

Mobile's Cathedral Parish began in 1703 and was housed in a modest church through the 18th century. The Cathedral Basilica of the Immaculate Conception was designed in 1833 and opened to the public in 1850. The portico was added in the 1870s and the towers were completed in 1884.

Unloading Bananas, Mobile, Ala.

Handcolored.

A hand-colored postcard of the port of Mobile. Refrigerated ships and railcars made the trade in bananas possible after 1900, and Mobile was one of the ports where the fruit was transferred from ship to train. United Fruit Company developed a complicated network to deliver bananas all over the country.

17

5207
Wreckage at foot of
St. Anthony St.,
Mobile, Ala.
Storm of
Sept. 27th, 1906.

Souvenir from
Hotel Woodbound,
Magnolia Springs,
Baldwin Co., Ala.

The hurricane of September 27, 1906, caused $15 million in damage in Mobile alone, mostly from an 11.6-foot storm surge that is still a record. There were only a few fatalities in Mobile. It was felt that the city withstood the storm reasonably well.

18

The Surrender Oak marked where the last Confederate army east of the Mississippi capitulated on May 4, 1865. On that day, Confederate Lt. Gen. Richard Taylor surrendered to Federal Maj. Gen. E. R. S. Canby. The site is now preserved as a small park.

Under this tree the last surrender of the Civil War took place, including 9000 troops of Alabama, Mississippi and east Louisiana, with their munitions of war; Lieut. Gen'l. Richard Taylor to Maj. Gen'l. Edward R. S. Canby, on May 4, 1865. (This tree was blown down in September, 1906.)

Surrender Oak, Citronelle, Alabama

═ BALDWIN COUNTY ═

Beach and Casino, Fairhope, Ala,

The beaches and entertainment venues at Fairhope transformed the community into a vacation destination in the early 1900s. Drawn by the town's utopian origins, famous intellectuals such as Upton Sinclair, Sherwood Anderson, and Wharton Esherick were among its visitors.

The Pier and Beach, Fairhope, Ala.

The Fairhope pier was originally built in 1894. Considered the "town square" by Fairhope's residents, the pier was destroyed by Hurricane Katrina and rebuilt in 2006.

Miflin is a small town in Baldwin County, south of Foley and Elberta. It was incorporated and had a post office, shown in the picture, in the first half of the 20th century.

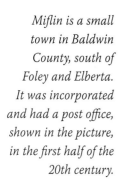

20

Foley School Auditorium
Foley, Alabama

The Foley School Auditorium was built in 1929 and was used until 2009. The building still stands on the Foley Middle School campus.

Elberta is a small town in southern Baldwin County, about ten miles east of the Florida border.

MAGNOLIA RIVER - MAGNOLIA SPRINGS, ALA.

Magnolia Springs, located in Baldwin County, was part of a Spanish land grant in 1800. The Magnolia River is the last remaining U.S. mail route to make deliveries by water.

The third version of the Point Clear Hotel, shown here, sits on the same site as the first hotel, built in 1875, and the second, built in 1947. It is one of the most popular resorts in the area.

Grand Hotel, Point Clear, Alabama 122

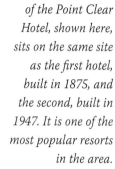

22

Main Dining Room, Grand Hotel, Point Clear, Ala.

The dining room of the Grand Hotel around the 1940s. After World War II, Edward A. Roberts renovated the hotel's facilities, adding golf courses, a pool, tennis courts, and a marina.

GULF STATE PARK CASINO

Gulf State Park's "Dance Casino", actually used for dining and dancing, not gambling, was built in 1939, soon after the land for the park was acquired by the state.

FOLEY HOTEL — FOLEY, ALABAMA

8B-H27

The Foley Hotel devoted the second floor to hotel rooms, and the first floor to retail businesses. Stacey's drug store was located in the space to the right of the entrance.

The Beach Hotel opened in the early 1900s and by 1907 guests arrived by ship to enjoy the three-story, bayside building. The original structure burned in 1930.

24

The steamboat in the background is the Jas. A. Carney, one of the "bay boats" which ferried passengers and cargo across Mobile Bay before a bridge was built in 1927. The Carney sank during the 1916 hurricane and was uniquely sunk by ice in 1898. Fortunately, it was always recovered and put back into service.

Court House, Bay Minette, Ala.

5420—89

The Baldwin County Courthouse in Bay Minette was built in 1900 by architect Frank Lockwood and contractor F. M. Dobson. It was remodeled in 1955 and again in 1996. The modern courthouse does not much resemble this one, but it does retain the clock.

25

BRODBECK & ZUNDEL BROS. GENERAL MERCHANDISE.

POST OFFICE, POINT CLEAR, ALA.

The Brodbeck & Zundel Brothers General Store, opened in 1866, served Point Clear as store and post office. It sold many types of merchandise, including lumber, which was shipped from Mississippi on a boat called The Lottie.

Summerdale is a small rural town in Baldwin County. Liveries allowed individuals to board their horses in a stable or field, and in some instances they rented horses for use in travel and farming.

Elberta was founded in 1903 by the Baldwin County Colonization Company to take advantage of the area's timber tracts. The company began building a town for the German immigrants recruited to the area, and the first hotel was opened in 1904.

≈ ESCAMBIA COUNTY ≈

Main Street, looking North, Flomaton, Ala.

Flomaton was incorporated as a town in 1908 and sits at a railway junction. The name is a portmanteau of "Florida," "Alabama," and "town."

ARENDS HOUSE, BREWTON, ALA.

The Arends Hotel was built in 1881 by John N. Arends. The postcard shows the hotel and guests around 1910.

Belleville Avenue, Looking North, Brewton, Ala.

Belleville Avenue was a residential street intersecting St. Joseph Avenue, where the historic business district of Brewton is located. This view shows the street as it appeared before 1925, when the first paved roads were laid in the town.

An early view of South Pensacola Street, still a major thoroughfare in Atmore. The picture probably dates to the 1910s, since telephone and electric wires— clearly visible here— were installed in 1908 (telephone) and 1914 (electricity).

SOUTH PENSACOLA AVENUE, ATMORE, ALA.

RESIDENCE OF W. Y. LOVELACE, BREWTON, ALABAMA

William Yancey Lovelace (1864–1933) was Brewton's mayor 1903–07. He and his brothers E. M. and J. A. owned between themselves or partnered in a lumber company, gin, oil mill, and the Lovelace Hotel. W. Y.'s grand residence was built about 1910.

29

Universalist Church,   Brewton, Alabama   24

The Brewton Universalist Church used this building until the 1980s. It is now the home of the Cornerstone Community Church of God. In the 1940s, the Universalists established the town's first public library.

FLOMATON BUS STATION CAFE
Flomaton, Alabama

The Flomaton Bus Depot and Cafe stood at the intersection of U.S. Highways 31 and 29. The cafe's slogan was "Where Friends Meet and the Hungry Eat."

30

Founded in 1911 as a rare college preparatory boarding school for African Americans, the Southern Normal School operated after 1919 as a permanent mission of the Reformed Church in America. In 1997, the school became known as the Southern Normal Academy of Alabama State University.

LOUNGE, KITTELL HALL,
SOUTHERN NORMAL SCHOOL, BREWTON, ALABAMA

The Williams Motel stood one mile north of Dothan on U.S. Highway 231. The slogan printed on this card referenced local pride that a fourth of the U.S. peanut crop was harvested and processed in and around Dothan.

Dothan's Foster Street, circa 1940. The movie theater is long gone, but the avenue is still the heart of downtown Dothan and hosts an annual street festival.

The congregation of First Baptist Church organized in 1887 in a simple one-room structure. In 1893, contractor H. H. Brown broke ground for new church at Main and Oates. The new church was admired for its woodwork, paneled ceiling, and stained-glass windows, but by 1927 it also was too small and was replaced.

First Baptist Church, Dothan, Ala

32

Prior to the interstate system, motels and motor courts served millions of (white) travelers along Southern highways. This one stood on U.S. 231, two miles north of Dothan. The back of the postcard boasted of on-site telephone and telegraph service.

KAT-O-LOG MOTEL COURT
DOTHAN, ALABAMA

First Methodist Church, Dothan, Ala.

The First Methodist Church of Dothan began as a brush arbor meeting in 1880 and organized into a church in 1881. This building was constructed in 1903–04 by J. C. Ward. It was in use until 1949.

PORTER'S FAIRY-LAND, DOTHAN, ALABAMA   112-D

FAIRYLAND

PHOTO BY THE RAINER STUDIO

Porter's Fairy-Land, about three miles east of Dothan off U.S. 84, was a popular hangout spot for Dothan's white teenagers. The facility had a dance area and a year-round swimming pool. Season tickets were coveted.

The County Courthouse was built in 1905, soon after Dothan became the seat of newly created Houston County. Andrew J. Bryan was the architect and M. T. Lewman and Company the contractor. It remained in use until replaced in 1962.

34

Dr. Earl Moody opened a private hospital in a small wooden building in Dothan in 1913. He expanded to this facility in 1919. The first penicillin given to an Alabamian was reportedly administered here in 1946. The hospital closed in the 1960s.

The Dothan Federal Building and United States Courthouse was built in 1911 under the supervision of architect Oscar Wenderoth. It is on the National Register of Historic Places and remains in use as the courthouse for the Middle District of Alabama, Southern Division.

35

Aerial photograph of Dothan in the first half of the 20th century. The view shows the mixed industrial and residential use that developed after Dothan gained railroad service in 1893.

HOUSTON HOTEL, DOTHAN, ALA.—9

Its towering eight floors and 150 rooms made the Houston Hotel (1928) one of Dothan's most recognizable landmarks. In 1974, the building became the campus of Troy State University at Dothan and was used by the college until 1990. The studios of WTVY were moved into the building in 1993.

36

This is home and home is not something you remember, it is something you see every day and every moment.

— RICK BRAGG, *Ava's Man, 2001*

Dale County Court House
Ozark, Alabama

The Dale County Courthouse was built in 1901. Andrew J. Bryan was the architect and M. T. Lewman was the contractor. It was torn down and replaced on the same site in 1966.

114-D

BUSINESS SECTION, OZARK, ALABAMA

37

A 1944 view of Ozark's town center, which is known for its antebellum commercial buildings and the Confederate monument visible in the middleground. Notice the red bricks of the courthouse, compared to the stylized rendering in the top card on this page.

112—On the March, Camp Rucker, Ala.

Camp Rucker, originally for infantry training and known as the Ozark Triangular Division Camp, expanded in September 1942 to accommodate a new airfield, now Cairns Army Airfield. Rucker was deactivated in 1946 and reopened during the Korean War.

38

104—Divisional Headquarters, Camp Rucker, Ala.

The Divisional Headquarters at Camp Rucker, 1943–44. Even the headquarters was a simple frame building, attesting to how quickly the camp facilities were built in order to contribute to the war effort. Beginning in early 1942, 15,000 buildings were erected in 106 days.

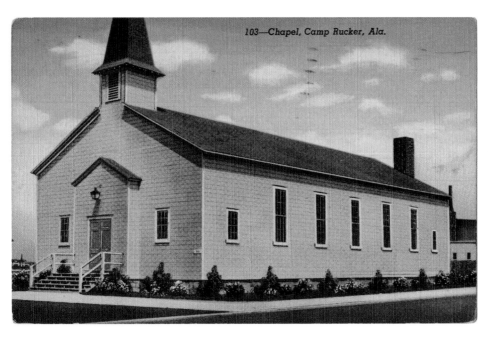

103—Chapel, Camp Rucker, Ala.

The Camp Rucker chapel circa 1945. Rucker, located in Dale and Coffee counties, was built on marginal farmland the federal government had bought during the Great Depression. During the War four infantry divisions trained here. The camp is named for Confederate Col. Edmund Rucker.

321ST INFANTRY REGIMENT ON FULL FIELD INSPECTION, CAMP RUCKER, ALA.   132-D

PHOTO BY THE PUBLIC RELATIONS OFFICE
81ST DIV., CAMP RUCKER, ALA.

The 321st Infantry Regiment was part of the 81st Infantry Division during World War II. The unit fought in the Pacific Theater, helping retake the Philippines from occupying Japan.

During World War II, the 81st, 35th, 98th, and 66th infantry divisions, as well as smaller units, trained at Camp Rucker. This postcard gives photo credit to the U.S. Army Signal Corps which was established in the 1830s and expanded during World War II to include photography and film making.

117—Various U. S. Field Artillery Activities, Camp Rucker, Ala.

PHOTOS BY U. S. ARMY SIGNAL CORPS

© CURT TEICH & CO., INC.

40

Service clubs (a base as large as Rucker would have had several) provided entertainment and leisure activities for officers and soldiers. The University of Michigan alumni newsletter reported that its 1941 alum Ransom S. Hawley was in charge of one of Rucker's service clubs and had developed a library of 5,000 books.

No. 688   SERVICE CLUB—CAMP RUCKER, ALABAMA

SOUTH ALABAMA

S. C. 15723

1910 Brock Hotel, C. C. Brock, Prop., Samson, Ala.

The Brock Hotel was a substantial building for the small town of Samson in Geneva County and played a central role from the early to the mid-20th century. In 1912, the Florala Boy Scouts hiked to the Brock, where they enjoyed tea and sandwiches. Judge and Mrs. J. P. Faulk Jr. wed in the hotel on February 14, 1931.

JAS. E. MOSELEY & CO.

G. Y. P. LUMBER CO., GENEVA, ALA.

Geneva County was created in 1868. Its virgin longleaf pine forests made turpentining and lumbering a key industry in the county. The company pictured was one of several local sawmills producing railroad crossties and "rough and dressed yellow pine" lumber.

HIGH SCHOOL, ENTERPRISE, ALA.

The Enterprise Public School was completed in 1906; it had seven classrooms, two offices, and a 600-seat auditorium. In 1907 it was deeded to the state as Coffee County High School, with grades 8–10. The building was rebuilt and expanded after a 1911 fire and served until replaced in 1955.

42

MONUMENT TO THE BOLL WEEVIL, ENTERPRISE, ALABAMA

2E-13

By 1910, the boll weevil had decimated Alabama's cotton production, forcing farmers to diversify with new crops. Enterprise and the surrounding area rebounded with the nation's largest peanut crop. In 1919, the appreciative citizens dedicated what is believed to be the only monument to an insect.

Residence of W. S. Harlan, Lockhart, Ala.

Covington County businessman W. S. Harlan is chiefly remembered for building a one-room schoolhouse for the town of Lockhart in 1924. The elementary school is still called the W. S. Harlan School. Lockhart was a company town for the Jackson Lumber Company, which closed in 1940.

FLORALA, ALA.

VERANDA COLONIAL HOTEL

VIEW OF LAKE JACKSON FROM COLONIAL HOTEL

Florala is so named because it sits near the Florida-Alabama line. Drawn to the area after the Civil War by cheap land, temperate climate, and abundant pine forests, early settlers built houses with wide porches overlooking the 500-acre Jackson Lake, formed by the collapse of limestone caves.

43

Shown here are Florala's first hospital, a residential street, and the main business street. Lake Jackson, bottom left, is named for Andrew Jackson, who camped overnight here in May 1818 on his way to Pensacola with 1,200 soldiers to engage the Spanish and their Native American allies.

44

Florala's Colonial Hotel opened in 1906 and was separated from Lake Jackson by railroad tracks that allowed guests to disembark directly at the hotel. The hotel was demolished in the 1980s to make room for the Bank of Florala.

BAPTIST CHURCH, EVERGREEN, ALA.

Founded in 1845, the Evergreen Baptist Church built the pictured sanctuary in 1908 and still occupies the building today. The congregation was instrumental in the founding of the Alabama Baptist Children's Home in 1891.

45

W.C. Crumpton Residence, Evergreen, Ala.

The home of state senator and judge advocate general W. C. Crumpton, around 1910. The home is an example of the Queen Anne style of architecture which was popular in the late 19th century. The asymmetrical design, front-facing gable, and octagonal tower are typical characteristics.

The Evergreen Hotel, at West Front and Rural streets, was operated by Cadwallader Beale. This postcard unusually advertises not just the hotel, but collotype printing, which was common in the late 19th century.

46

Evergreen was founded in 1819 when Revolutionary War veterans settled in the area. It was officially incorporated as a city in 1873.

Richmond Cedar Works, Greenville, Ala.

Greenville, in Butler County, is about 40 miles south of Montgomery. Wood processing was an important part of its early economy. This mill processed cedar logs which were shipped to the Richmond (Va.) Cedarworks Company to be made into products such as ice cream churns and cedar chests.

GREENVILLE BOOK AND STATIONERY CO.

Commerce Street. Greenville, Ala.

Greenville's main avenue, Commerce Street, passed through this substantial residential section as well as the town's main business district. The columned house on the right was the home of Judge J. K. Henry.

47

Like many other motels of the period, Troy's Hotel Watkins seems to have begun as a residence, a "tourist home" similar to later bed and breakfast establishments. The hotel offered "pure Artesian water," private garages, and a putting green.

HOTEL WATKINS AND ESTENCREST SERVICE STATION, TROY, ALA.

48

In 1887, the Alabama Legislature established Troy State Normal School to train teachers. Renamed State Normal College in 1893, the school in Pike County is known today as Troy University.

State Normal College, Troy, Ala.

Pike County Court House, Troy, Ala.

This structure in Troy was completed in 1881 and renovated in 1898. It served as the Pike County Courthouse until it was demolished and replaced in 1953. Visible behind the courthouse is the store of J. P. Wood, who is listed in the 1910 census as a hardware merchant.

North Three Notch Street, Troy, Ala.

In 1824, U.S. Army Captain Daniel Burch laid out the Three Notch Road from Fort Barrancas in Pensacola, Florida, to Fort Mitchell in Russell County, Alabama. Ostensibly for moving military supplies, the road was used by settlers moving into Alabama and Florida.

Commercial establishments on U.S. 231 between Troy and Montgomery. The Pine Lake Motel still stands, though it is now part of a motel chain. Saxon's began as an Alabama candy company; by the mid-1950s, its 40 locations included restaurants and gift shops.

50

U.S. 231 runs from St. John, Indiana, to Panama City, Florida. Prior to the interstate system, Highway 231 was heavily trafficked and lined with hundreds of motels, motor courts, cafes, and drive-in restaurants.

MOTEL PLAZA
U. S. 231 Inside City
Troy, Alabama

Stewart Warner Saf-Aire Heat

"White Way," Broad Street, Eufaula, Ala.

Originally named Irwinton, Eufaula was incorporated in 1857 and became prosperous off shipping along the Chattahoochee River. The Seth Lore and Irwinton Historic District, which includes Broad Street, is the second largest historic district in Alabama.

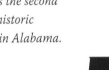

51

McDowell Bridge, Chattahoochee River, Eufaula, Alabama

The McDowell Bridge was built in 1925 through the combined efforts of Alabama, Georgia, and the federal government. It was named for Charles S. McDowell, lieutenant governor of Alabama 1923–27, who had advocated for the project.

OB873-N

The Shorter Mansion was built in 1884 by Eli Shorter, a lawyer and Congressman, and his wife, Wileyna Lamar Shorter, heiress to a patent medicine fortune. Craftsmen were brought in to create the woodwork and other elaborate features of the house, which remained in the Shorter family until 1968. It is now a house museum.

Shorter Mansion, Eufaula, Ala.

Eufaula is one of the oldest towns in the state. Bordered by ancient trees and imposing houses, Eufaula Street (now Eufaula Avenue) is the historic district which draws tourists to the town. Many of the structures are on the National Register of Historic Places.

Eufaula Street, Eufaula, Ala.

≈ MONTGOMERY COUNTY ≈

State Capitol, Montgomery, Alabama

Alabama's Capitol overlooks downtown Montgomery from a site informally called "Goat Hill." The main part of the structure was built in 1850–51, over the foundations of the1848 capitol that burned in 1850. The Capitol was designated a National Historic Landmark in 1960.

Commerce Street and "Slogan" Sign by Night, Montgomery, Ala.

Lower Commerce Street, leading from the Alabama River to Court Square, and lined with elaborate warehouses, was the heart of Montgomery's business life. In 1909, a large electric sign proclaiming "Montgomery—Key to Your Opportunity" was placed to greet arriving train passengers.

Jefferson Davis Home, Montgomery, Ala.

The first "White House of the Confederacy" was on the corner of Bibb and Washington streets when the Jefferson Davis family lived in it in early 1861. Afterwards, it was a residence and boarding house before being moved near the Capitol in 1918 and restored as a house museum.

54

MASONIC HOME, MONTGOMERY, ALA.—9

Opened in 1912 off Carter Hill Road near present-day Montgomery Academy, the Masonic Home was for the care of widows and orphans of deceased master Masons and for Masons who could no longer take care of themselves. In its early days, the Home included a school.

The Whitley Hotel on Montgomery Street, next-door to the Paramount Theatre, which offered moving pictures and live performances. Lauren Bacall was a guest when she brought her tap dance act to the Paramount. Today, the Whitley is the main hall of Troy University's Montgomery campus.

In 1899, Montgomery officials purchased 45 acres that became Oak Park. In the background of the postcard is the original pavilion that was demolished in 1937 and replaced with a granite structure. A civil rights lawsuit in the 1960s ended racial segregation in the park.

55

County Court House. Montgomery. Ala.

The second Montgomery County Courthouse was built in 1854 by architect Charles C. Ordeman. It was enlarged in 1894, then torn down and replaced on the same site in the mid-1950s. The replacement was demoted to an annex when the fourth courthouse was built in 1987.

56

St. Peters Catholic Church, Montgomery, Ala.

St. Peter's was the first Roman Catholic Church in Montgomery. Its first building was erected in 1834 at the corner of Lawrence and Adams streets. It was replaced on the same site by the present edifice in 1852–53. This postcard photo seems to have been taken before stained-glass windows were installed in 1922.

The original Exchange Hotel was demolished in 1904 and this one (left center) was erected on the same site in 1906, across from downtown's tallest building, First National Bank. The streetcar passing the fountain was on the "Lightning Route," the first city-wide system of electric streetcars in the U.S.

57

Montgomery City Hall burned in 1932 and was replaced on the same site at Monroe and Perry; many city documents and records were lost in the fire. The three-story building had a city market at ground level, offices on the second floor, and a municipal auditorium on the top floor.

POST OFFICE, MONTGOMERY, ALA.

A post office was erected in 1884 at the corner of Dexter and Lawrence by builder Lewis Owen. Children lined up for rides on its elevator, the first in Montgomery. The fine-quality stone used for the foundation was quarried in Alabama.

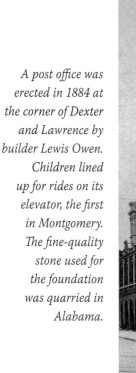

58

The road I took out more than forty years ago is still two-way and now beckons me to return. . . . This is the place and these are the people that made me what I am. . . . In order to know myself, I must return to where I started.

— WADE HALL, *Conecuh People*

Woman's College of Alabama, Montgomery, Ala.

Huntington College, Montgomery, Ala.

7A-H3255

The two postcards on this page offer strikingly different views of the same structure—Flowers Memorial Hall—on the campus of what is now Huntingdon College. Originally Tuskegee Female College, it relocated to Montgomery in 1908 as the Woman's College of Alabama. The college graduated its first male student in 1934 and renamed itself again, this time in honor of Selina, Countess of Huntingdon, an early Methodist leader (and a cousin of George Washington). Flowers Hall was designed by Harvard-trained architect H. Langford Warren in the Gothic style of the buildings of Oxford and Cambridge colleges.

59

Named for a former governor, Kilby Prison cost $2,250,000—more than the total of all other prisons in the state up to that time. Inmates worked at a self-contained cotton mill, shirt factory, and 100-cow dairy. Considered state-of-the-art when built in 1923, by 1970 it was dilapidated and had to be razed.

Cramton Bowl was a baseball stadium when it opened in 1922; local businessman Fred Cramton donated the land. Baseball moved across Madison Avenue after Paterson Field was built, and since then Cramton Bowl has hosted football, including the first game played in the South under electric lights, in 1927.

CRAMTON BOWL

A romanticized night view of downtown Montgomery, looking south from Commerce Street, across Court Square with the fountain in the center and the Winter Building just beyond. In the background are the county courthouse and Sidney Lanier High School (now Baldwin).

U. S. NATIONAL GUARD—CAMP SHERIDAN, MONTGOMERY, ALA.

2026 The Mess Halls of the Boys of the National Guard.
C. UNDERWOOD & UNDERWOOD

Bird's Eye View by Night, Montgomery, Ala.

Camp Sheridan was established in July 1917 to train National Guardsmen for World War I service. The name honored Union Civil War general Philip H. Sheridan, but Montgomery merchants were glad to supply the Ohioans in the 37th U.S. Infantry Division, who served in France 1917–18.

The Bell Building was constructed by N. J. Bell. When completed in 1907, the 187-foot "skyscraper" was the tallest structure in Montgomery. It was designed by Frederick Ausfeld, a native of Austria who became a prominent Montgomery architect. The Bell Building had three Otis steam elevators with brass and polished wood cars. The building is still in use and is on the National Register of Historic Places.

62

"Negro and white . . . neighborhoods adjoined. . . . But each section turned its back on its neighbor and faced into its own community for its social and cultural life."

— MARTIN LUTHER KING JR., *Stride Toward Freedom: The Montgomery Story*

M-8—Governor's Mansion
Montgomery, Alabama

This large home on South Perry Street is the second official residence of Alabama's governors. Built in 1907 by Robert F. Ligon Jr., it was purchased by the state in 1950 for $100,000. Every governor since Gordon Persons has lived there.

63

The Wharf, Alabama River, Montgomery, Ala.

Montgomery's first white settlers established a landing on the Alabama River at the foot of what became Commerce Street. The first steamboat, The Harriet, *arrived from Mobile in 1821. A new wharf and a cotton slide were soon built.*

The first Confederate offices were in this building, which later housed the Majestic Theater and a popular restaurant, the Pickwick. The building burned in 1926. Next door was a furniture store owned by Frank Tennille, a former big-band singer who had returned to run his family business.

64

Maxwell Field got its start in 1910, when the Wright brothers established a short-lived flying school on the Kohn plantation northwest of the city. During World War I, the Army leased the site for a repair depot. In the 1920s, it became a permanent installation. In the center is Austin Hall, built in 1930 as the base's first educational building.

UNION STATION, MONTGOMERY, ALA.

Union Station opened in 1898; it was built by the L&N Railroad but served several lines. At one time 40 trains a day came through Montgomery, but by the 1970s rail traffic had declined and the station closed. It was later renovated and houses a city welcome center and commercial tenants.

Knights of Pythias Childrens' Home,
Montgomery, Ala.-33

The Knights of Pythias fraternal organization was strong in Alabama in the early 1900s, with many prominent Alabamaians as members. Around 1920 the national organization urged state divisions to establish homes for widows, orphans, and indigent Pythians. By 1923 this one opened.

Dexter Avenue Methodist Church, Montgomery, Ala.

Methodists built this Richardsonian Romanesque-style church, designed by R. W. McGrath, on Dexter Avenue in 1896. It was especially noted for its round-headed windows and doors and its fine decorative brickwork, done by J. B. Worthingdon. The building has had extensive remodeling over the years but is still used by a non-denominational congregation.

66

One persistent element of southern folklore sought to explain the variations in denominations: a Methodist was a Baptist who wore shoes; a Presbyterian was a Methodist with a bank account.

— WAYNE FLYNT, *Poor but Proud: Alabama's Poor Whites*

G 16123 Court Square,
         Montgomery, Ala.

Copyright 1904 by the Ro...

Cotton season on a foggy morning, Montgomery, Ala.

Electric trolley cars and Court Square Fountain are in the foreground of this depiction of the Moses Building, Montgomery's first skyscraper. It was built in 1887 and demolished in 1907. The fountain was built in 1885 and is topped by a statue of Hebe, the "Goddess of Youth and Cupbearer to the Gods."

67

Cotton and slaves were the two commodities that fueled Montgomery's economy prior to the Civil War, and cotton continued to be vital into the 20th century. This view looks down Commerce Street toward the Alabama River.

THE AIR-CONDITIONED DINKLER-JEFFERSON DAVIS

PETITE CAFE

The Jefferson Davis Hotel opened in 1927. It was also home to the WFSA studio where Hank Williams started his career in the 1930s and 1940s. It was added to the National Register of Historic Places in 1979. Today it serves as a senior citizen and low-income apartment house.

68

M-27—Dexter Avenue, Looking East, Showing State Capitol, Montgomery, Ala.

The basin at Court Square was a watering hole for livestock and a central meeting place and slave auction site from Montgomery's earliest days. The statue in the center of the basin was put into place on April 30, 1886. It was cast by the J. L. Mott Iron Works of New York.

LEE COUNTY

Lee County Court House, Opelika, Ala.—5

Opelika - Ala.

After the Civil War, the Alabama Legislature carved a new county from four adjacent counties and named it after Robert E. Lee. This second courthouse—since modified but still in use—was built in Opelika, the county seat, in 1896 across the street from the 1867 original, which was demolished.

Opelika, Ala. South Railroad Street, W. E. Palmer, OPELIKA, Ala.

The Montgomery and West Point Railroad Company extended a line to the small town of Opelika in the 1840s. By the mid-1850s, the town had become a hub for shipments of cotton; in the 20th century, it developed a thriving textile mill industry.

Aerial View of Main Campus Section, Alabama Polytechnic Institute, Auburn, Ala.

Lee County's most famous institution began in 1856 as the Methodist-affiliated East Alabama Male College, later known as Alabama Polytechnic Institute, and today as Auburn University. In 1872, the school became a state land grant university.

Alabama Polytechnic built its first separate library building in 1908, with a grant from Andrew Carnegie. It served students until the Draughon Library opened in 1963. The Carnegie Library was remodeled and renamed Mary Martin Hall, honoring a beloved former librarian.

Library, A. P. I., Auburn, Ala.

PRESIDENT'S HOME, ALABAMA POLYTECHNIC INSTITUTE, AUBURN, ALA.

5879-29

The 1915 Old President's Mansion was the residence of Auburn presidents until 1938. Renovated and renamed Katharine Cooper Cater Hall, it now houses education support services.

71

Eight Street, Opelika, Ala

Eighth Street runs through Opelika's historic downtown district. This card is postmarked 1909, so the scene is earlier; wagons and bicycles are visible, but no automobiles, and the street appears unpaved. The middle building on the left may be a hotel, with bedding hung out to air.

Some 3,000 persons attended the April 6, 1911 dedication of a Confederate Monument sponsored by the Robert E. Lee Chapter of the United Daughters of the Confederacy. "Comrades" and "To our Confederate veterans" are inscribed on the base, below two crossed flags and the date, "1861–1865."

CONFEDERATE MONUMENT, OPELIKA, ALA.   3450

The Hotel Clement, on the corner of South 9th Street and Avenue A, opened in 1910 and operated until 1969. In its heyday it offered the area's finest accommodations, as well as a fine dining room. The site is now the home of the Museum of East Alabama.

HOTEL CLEMENT
Opelika, Alabama
Recommended by Duncan Hines

Talladega College
Talladega, Ala.

Talladega College, founded in 1865 by ex-slaves, is Alabama's oldest private historically black college. On the left is Foster Hall, built in 1869 as a girls' dormitory. In the foreground is DeForest Chapel, built in 1903 and named for Henry Swift DeForest, the college's second president.

Savery Library, Talladega College, Talladega, Alabama

9A348-N

Savery Library, built in 1939, is named for William Savery, one of the ex-slave founders. The library holds the famous Hale Woodruff murals depicting the rebellion of captured Africans being transported into slavery aboard a sailing ship, the Amistad.

73

Andrews Hall was built in 1909 to replace Graves Hall, which burned in that year. The new structure was named after Reverend George Whitfield Andrews, dean of the Theological Department from 1875 to 1908.

A Purefoy Hotel operated in Monroeville from 1916 to 1920, but a new 88-room version opened in Talladega on May 17, 1920. The hotel was known for the offerings in its fine dining room, especially the pecan pie.

TALLADEGA, ALA.
ELKS HALL AND THEATRE.

S. H. Henderson & Co.

Talladega's Elks Theatre was built in the early 20th century, and, for its time, was modern in every respect, even lit by electricity. Evening attire was expected of patrons in the dress circle and box seats. The theater was the venue for many traveling shows, plays, operas, and local events.

Synodical College for Women, Talladega, Ala.

A school for some 75 years, this 1851 building contained a chapel, library, and classrooms. It was named Presbyterian Collegiate Female Institute, later Institute Female College, then Isbell College for Young Ladies, and from 1903 to 1925, Alabama Synodical College for Women. Afterwards, it was a hospital.

Sylacauga sits atop a substantial deposit of highly prized white marble, explaining the city's nickname, "the Marble City." Quarries opened as early as the mid-19th century, but developed in earnest in the 1880s and into the early 1900s. Sylacauga marble was used in the construction of the Lincoln Memorial, the United States Supreme Court, the Alabama Department of Archives and History, and many other important buildings in the state and nation.

ALABAMA MARBLE QUARRY, SYLACAUGA, ALABAMA—3

76

From the quarries where thy marble, White as that of Pharos gleams, Waiting till the sculptor's chisel, Wakes to life the poet's dreams . . .

— JULIA TUTWILER (lyrics to "Alabama," the state song)

Salt Creek Falls is located in the Talladega National Forest near the community of Hopeful. The water cascades through a natural amphitheater of high cliffs, forming a popular swimming hole at the bottom. Access is hazardous because of the steep climb in and out over the rocks.

77

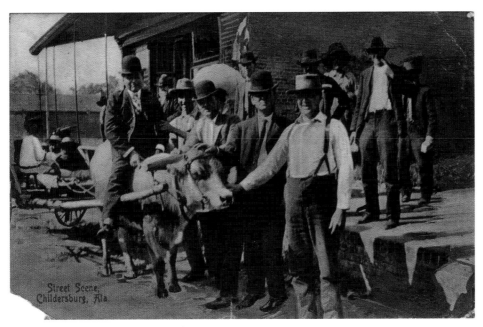

Childersburg calls itself "the Oldest City in America," due to its status as a Coosa village when Spanish explorer Hernando de Soto traveled through Alabama in 1540. Whites began to settle the area in the 1830s and developed timber and charcoal industries.

HIGH SCHOOL, SYLACAUGA, ALABAMA 3312

In 1895, the legislature created the District Agricultural School and Experiment Station, Sylacauga's first public high school. It was renamed Sylacauga High and moved into this new building in 1923. The building has been modified and expanded several times and remains in use.

78

Lincoln was incorporated as a town in 1911 and shortly afterward was chosen as the site for a new Talladega County High School.

Talladega County High School, Lincoln ,Ala.

DALLAS COUNTY

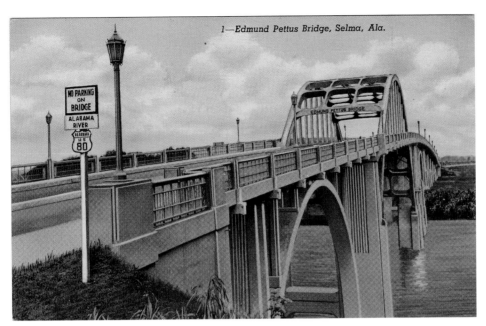

1—Edmund Pettus Bridge, Selma, Ala.

The Edmund Pettus Bridge, famous as the site of the 1965 "Bloody Sunday" attack on civil rights marchers, opened in 1940. Designed by Henson Stephenson, the 250-foot steel "through arch" bridge carries traffic on U.S. Highway 80 over the Alabama River.

6—Broad Street, Looking North, Selma, Ala.

In the 1950s, Selma's downtown business district remained one of the busiest in Alabama. Stores visible in this 1950s view of Broad Street include Pilcher-McBride Drug Company, Tepper's and Lilienthal's department stores, and Tillman Drugs.

In 1950, prayer meetings were held on Thursday nights in Selma's Elkdale Park. Named The Elkdale Prayer Group, these meetings grew to become the Elkdale Baptist Church.

80

This house on Alabama Avenue was the home of Edmund W. Pettus (1821–1907), a lawyer, Confederate general, civic leader, important figure in local and state politics, U. S. Senator, and reputed KKK leader. Today he is mostly known because of the bridge that bears his name.

DALLAS COUNTY COURT HOUSE AND ANNEX, SELMA, ALA.   119812

The Dallas County Courthouse in Selma was completed in 1901; the architect was Walter Chamberlain, and J. W. Hood was the contractor. The annex to the right was added in 1910. The building was remodeled in 1959, just in time for voting rights demonstrations in the 1960s.

King's Sanitarium, Selma, Ala.

Selma's first private hospital was founded in 1896 by Dr. Goldsby King, who had studied at Johns Hopkins and the University of Heidelburg. He served as city physician and county health officer. He died in 1920, but his sanitarium operated until 1953. It is now Ellwood Community Church's "Circle of Love Center."

81

On the left is the Hotel Albert, for many years a Selma landmark. Construction began in 1861 but was suspended during the war. It opened in 1867 but was not finished until 1892. It was demolished in 1959. Also visible are Hooper Insurance, Lloyd's Bakery, and Sears Roebuck.

14—Broad Street at Night, Looking South, Selma, Ala.

After the Civil War, competition among hotels in Selma was so fierce that the city council passed an ordinance fining anyone who "did harass any person arriving on railroads or steamboats for patronage or handling baggage."

Arcadia Hotel, Selma, Ala.

Alabama River, showing Draw Bridge open, Selma, Ala.

The Old "Swing Bridge" was built in 1884–85 by the Milwaukee Bridge Works. The north span was manually opened to let boats pass through the 100-foot space between the pillars, so a bridge tender was on duty around the clock. The Edmund Pettus Bridge replaced it in 1940.

83

Louisville and Nashville Passenger Depot, Selma, Ala.

This passenger depot in Selma was one of many stations used by the Louisiana and Nashville Railroad, which held a dominant position in Alabama railroading in 1900. Located on historic Water Avenue, today the L&N Passenger Depot in Selma is the Old Depot Museum.

The First Baptist Church of Selma was organized in 1842; the building was erected in 1904. Its High Victorian Gothic design includes a massive four-story tower decorated with gargoyles and stone tracery. The church building features a stained-glass window and mosaic tile designed by Selma native Carla Weaver Parrish and made by Tiffany and Co. of New York. Some of the other stained-glass windows were salvaged from the earlier church building.

84

21—First Baptist Church, Selma, Ala.

And I imagined that when [the Lord] came it would be like looking at the Baptist window: pretty as colored glass with the sun shining through, such a shine as you don't know it's getting dark.

— Truman Capote, "A Christmas Memory," 1958

TUSCALOOSA COUNTY

HISTORIC MONUMENT, SECOND STATE CAPITAL,
TUSCALOOSA, ALABAMA

Tuscaloosa was home to the state's second capital from 1826 to 1846. The building burned to the ground in 1923; the memorial reads, "This stone commemorates the city of Tuscaloosa as the second state capital, January 1826 to January 1846. Erected by the Alabama Centennial Commission and the Citizens of Tuscaloosa, and dedicated December 14, 1919, on the occasion of the one-hundredth anniversary of Alabama's admission to the Union of States."

And, believe me, to have been in the city of Tuscaloosa in October when you were young and full of Early Times and had a shining Alabama girl by your side, to have had all that . . . that was very good indeed.

— HOWELL RAINES, "Goodbye to the Bear," 1983

Construction on the President's Mansion began in 1839 and was completed in 1841 at the south end of the University of Alabama's quad. The house was designed by Michael Barry and was intended to complement the existing campus designed by William Nichols. The first president to live in the Mansion was Basil Manly.

These buildings are part of the Gorgas-Manly Historic District that includes five other campus buildings. Manly Hall was named for Dr. Basil Manly, the second president of the university; Clark Hall is named for Willis Clark, an early trustee. Woods Hall is named in honor of Alva Woods, the first president of the university.

86

T-11   PRESIDENT'S HOME, UNIVERSITY OF ALABAMA, TUSCALOOSA, ALA.

2A-H899

Quarter Angle, University of Alabama, Tuscaloosa, Ala.

Campus View, University of Alabama,
Tuscaloosa, Ala.—24

*This early view of
the University of
Alabama campus,
before the Gorgas
Library was built
in 1939, shows
the round house
on the left, and in
background, Manly,
Clark, and Garland
halls. The round
house is one of the
few buildings that
survived the burning
of the campus in the
Civil War.*

87

Denny Stadium, University of Alabama, Tuscaloosa, Ala.

*Now known as
Bryant-Denny
stadium, this field
was built in 1929
and named after
George Hutcheson
Denny, the 15th
president of the
university. The
original stadium
sat 12,000 and was
expanded in 1937 to
hold an additional
6,000.*

Originally called simply the "barracks" and made partially of bricks salvaged from Civil War destruction on the campus, Alva Woods Hall was the first new UA structure built (1867–68) after the war. It was renamed in 1884 in honor of the university's first president.

88

The University of Alabama's Morgan Hall was constructed in 1911 and built in the Beaux-Arts style out of Missouri yellow brick. Named after John Tyler Morgan, a U.S. Senator from 1876 to 1907, Morgan Hall housed the School of Law on the third floor from 1911–27, and today it is home to the Department of English.

Smith Hall, named in honor of state geologist Eugene Allen Smith, was built in 1907–10 to house the Museum of Natural History, as well as classrooms for several scientific departments. Built in Beaux-Arts style, Smith Hall faces Morgan Hall, a very similar building built to house humanities departments.

89

Comer Hall, named for Alabama Governor Braxton Bragg Comer, was built for the College of Engineering in 1909–10. It contained offices, classrooms, and the engineering library, as well as the university power plant which was located in the central part of the building.

Doster Hall, named for Dean of Education John Jarvis Doster, was built in 1929 for the School of Home Economics. It is still used today for classrooms and offices for what is now the College of Human Environmental Sciences.

90

The University of Alabama's Sorority Row is located around Magnolia Drive near University Boulevard. The area has undergone substantial redevelopment, with new and larger houses being built to replace those seen here. The first UA sorority was Kappa Delta.

FRATERNITY ROW, UNIVERSITY OF ALABAMA, TUSCALOOSA, ALA.—7

The first "fraternity row" was located on the west side of the campus, on University Boulevard toward downtown Tuscaloosa.

T-21 GYMNASIUM, UNIVERSITY OF ALABAMA, TUSCALOOSA, ALA.

2A-H909

Originally a boys' gymnasium named in honor of William "Bill" Gray Little, the student credited with bringing football to the campus in 1892, Little Hall was built in 1915. Today it houses the School of Social Work.

T-32—Aerial View of Alabama University, Tuscaloosa, Ala.

The University of Alabama, the state's oldest public university, opened on April 18, 1831, with 52 students and a campus that consisted of 7 buildings. Its undergraduate enrollment today is 42,000.

At left is Denny Chimes, the university's iconic landmark. The tower, named after President George Denny, was built in 1929. The 115-foot tower is located on the south side of the quad, beside University Boulevard.

UNIVERSITY OF
ALABAMA

(Check here)

☐ ARRIVED ON CAMPUS
☐ ROOMMATE IS GREAT
☐ MET MISS UNIVERSE
☐ PROFESSORS ARE THE MOST
☐ SAW NATION'S No. 1 FOOTBALL TEAM
☐ LOVE MY SORORITY SISTERS
☐ LIKE MY FRAT BROTHERS
☐ YOU SHOULD SEE MY DORM
☐ GOT LOST IN FIELD HOUSE
☐ SAW THE "BEAR"
☐ RAN OUT OF BLANK CHECKS

Other Reasons: ....
....

T-24 Barnwell Hall, "Girls' Gym" at University of Alabama, Tuscaloosa, Ala.

Barnwell Hall was built in 1930 as the women's gym. At that time an area south of what is now University Boulevard was known as the "Women's Campus," and the women's gym was located there. The building was named for former Dean of Arts and Sciences Charles H. Barnwell.

FARRAH HALL, SCHOOL OF LAW, UNIVERSITY OF ALABAMA, TUSCALOOSA, ALA.—48

Farrah Hall was constructed in 1927 and was the home of the School of Law until 1978. It was named for Law School Dean Albert J. Farrah. Since 1978 it has housed the university's Map Library, the graduate programs of the School of Social Work, and the Department of Criminal Justice.

Bryce Hospital (misspelled on card), built in Tuscaloosa in the 1850s, was the first mental health facility in the state, and was once among the world's largest. The first buildings—the cream-colored buildings in the center of the picture—were designed by physician Thomas Kirkbride.

94

The building used by Central Female College was built as Alabama's second State Capitol, but when the seat of state government moved to Montgomery in 1847 the property was deeded to the University of Alabama for educational purposes. The building burned in 1923.

Indian Mound, showing Part of Burial Ground, near Tuscaloosa

Moundville is an ancient archeological site of Mississippian culture that was occupied from 1000 AD to 1450 AD. The 300-acre village is characterized by large mounds that signified status within the Native American people's stratified society. It is the second largest site of its kind.

95

3353

MOBILE AND OHIO R. R. BRIDGE OVER WARRIOR RIVER, TUSCALOOSA, ALA.

The Mobile and Ohio Railroad Bridge over the Black Warrior River was built around 1910 by Benjamin H. Hardaway, constructing engineer. During the flood of 1951 the automobile bridge was impassible, so passengers were transported across the river on railroad flatcars.

Oak City Drug Co.   Broad St., Tuscaloosa, Ala.

Broad Street became University Boulevard after 1930. The Oak City Drug Company advertised in the 1910 Corolla, *the University of Alabama yearbook, and appeared in several professional directories of the period. The tall building at the center of the image is currently DePalma's restaurant.*

96

This house was built in 1837 by Dr. John R. Drish, a physician who owned a plantation outside Tuscaloosa. It combines features from the Italianate and the Greek Revival styles, and was used as a residence until 1906 when it was purchased by the Tuscaloosa Board of Education.

Jennison School, Tuscaloosa, Ala.

The McLester Hotel was built in 1887 at the intersection of Greensboro Avenue and Sixth Street. The three-story building had 33 rooms and the ground floor contained a store, an office, and a dining room.

97

Stafford School was Tuscaloosa's first public school. It was established in 1885 and occupied the former Alabama Female Institute, seen here. The building was located at 2209 9th Street and was demolished in 1955.

The sanitarium opened around 1912. In 1915, eight local doctors joined Dr. George A. Searcy and Dr. W. G. Sommerville and jointly operated the sanitarium as the Druid City Infirmary. A new building replaced the sanitarium in 1923 and was known as the Druid City Hospital.

THE SEARCY-SOMERVILLE SANITARIUM, TUSCALOOSA, ALA.

This courthouse was actually the sixth built in Tuscaloosa. It was completed in 1906 and was the first to be located on Greensboro Avenue. The architect was William Earnest Spink of Birmingham; contractors were Carrigan and Lynn. It opened in 1906 and was used until 1964.

TUSCALOOSA COUNTY COURT HOUSE, TUSCALOOSA, ALA.

Main Street in Greensboro, as depicted by Walker Evans in 1936. Most of the buildings still stand. Evans and James Agee visited Hale County on an assignment for Fortune *magazine that evolved into the 1941 classic book,* Let Us Now Praise Famous Men.

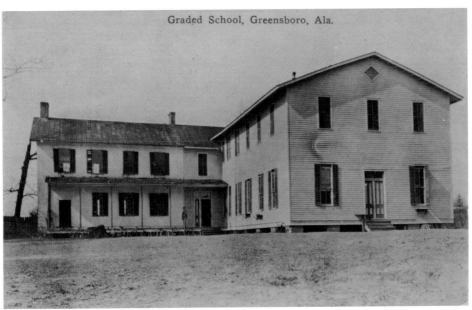

Graded School, Greensboro, Ala.

The Greensboro Graded School, on Demopolis Street, operated out of what was once the Greensboro Female Academy. The Academy closed in 1900 and the property was rented for use as a public school.

Southern University was established in Greensboro in 1856 by the Methodist church, dedicated to high academic standards and ideals of service. After a period of decline after the Civil War it flourished in the late 1800s, with a peak enrollment of 238 in 1889. It was destroyed by a tornado in 1973.

Eutaw, founded in 1834 and incorporated in 1841, is one of the oldest towns in the state. Wilson is one of its original streets, with at least ten sites on the National Register of Historic Places. The street is bordered by what seem to be white picket fences.

4330   ARTESIAN WELL, LIVINGSTON, ALA.

The artesian well, bored in 1854–57, was famous for the medicinal effects of its mineral waters. Livingston was considered a health resort well into the 20th century. The artesian well is known today as Bored Well and is located on Courthouse Square.

5166   ENNIS COUNTRY HOME, LIVINGSTON, ALA.   ILLUST. POST CARD CO., N. Y.

This house, known as Oak Manor, is an example of the I-type of plantation house, with a main block one room deep, and a narrow one-story section leading to a one-story kitchen. Other features of this house include a two-story veranda and an observatory on the roof. It was built around 1860.

WEBB HALL AND CAMPUS, STATE TEACHERS COLLEGE, LIVINGSTON, ALA.

Now the University of West Alabama, the college was officially Livingston State Teachers College from 1929 to 1957. The State Teachers College had the authority to grant a Bachelor of Science degree, with a Bachelor of Arts authorized in 1947.

102

Actually the Allen-Norwood Building, this commercial building originally had three storefront units. Located at 103 Washington Street in Demopolis, it was built in 1895. It is still in use; in recent years it has housed Spiller Furniture Company and Rutledge Drugs.

ALLEN NORWOOD BUILDING, SHOWING SIMMONS' DRUG STORE, DEMOPOLIS, ALA.

"OLD GAINESWOOD" AS IT LOOKED IN 1860, DEMOPOLIS, ALA.

Gaineswood is considered the finest remaining example of Greek Revival architecture in Alabama. The first house on the site was begun in 1843, a log building that was expanded into the Greek Revival mansion in 1861. It was designed by General Nathan Bryan Whitfield, who owned the estate 1843–61.

Tucker Drug Co. Pub.   LYON RESIDENCE, BLUFF HALL, DEMOPOLIS, ALA.

Bluff Hall was built in 1832 by Allen Glover for his daughter and her husband Francis Strother Lyon. It is located on White Bluff overlooking the Tombigbee River. It is now owned by the Marengo County Historical Commission and is maintained as a museum.

SCENE ON TOM BIGBEE RIVER, DEMOPOLIS, ALA.

The Tombigbee River was the regional center of commerce and trade of Alabama and Mississippi, transporting cotton, lumber, bacon, flour, and cornmeal. Steamboats appeared on the river in the 1820s and reigned on the Upper Tombigbee for nearly one hundred years.

104

A circa 1900 view of Washington Street, which runs through the heart of the Demopolis Historic Business District and adjoins the town square and city hall. W. J. Breitbach's Bargain Store can be seen on the right side of the street, advertising dry goods and shoes.

B71B3   Washington Street, Looking East, Demopolis, Ala.

MARION INSTITUTE, MARION, ALA.

110168

Marion Military Institute occupies a campus erected for the Howard English and Classical School, founded by the Alabama Baptist Convention in 1842. The Chapel (central building, with tower), built 1857, and Lovelace Hall, left side of card, built 1854, were used as a military hospital during the Civil War.

105

Water Street, Uniontown, Ala.

Uniontown, in Perry County, is one of the oldest towns in the state, first settled in 1818. This picture shows Uniontown's main business street, with some substantial commercial buildings but before the arrival of the automobile or electricity.

The main building at Judson, called Jewett Hall after Dr. Milo P. Jewett, the college's first president, is actually the third building of that name. The first Jewett Hall, built in 1840, was destroyed by fire in 1888 and was replaced by the second Jewett Hall, depicted here. It also burned, in 1940.

106

Cotton cultivation came early to Perry County; there was a cotton gin in Marion perhaps as early as 1817. The practice was to take the cotton to the gin once enough had been picked to make up a bale—about 500 pounds. In the picking season, wagons lined up at the gin each workday.

IKE'S MOTOR COURT and CAFE on U. S. Highway 31, 2 Miles north of Clanton, Alabama

Ike's Motor Court was located on U.S. Highway 31, a road that runs from Spanish Fort on the Gulf Coast to northern Michigan. In Alabama it was the main north-south route from Tennessee to Mobile. Clanton was located on the heavily used Birmingham-Montgomery stretch.

107

Loading Long Leaf Yellow Pine Logs. Twin Tree Lumber Co., Maplesville, Alabama.

The Twin Tree Lumber Company was active in Maplesville and in south Georgia in the early 20th century, specializing in yellow pine flooring. Longleaf yellow pine is used in lumber, pulp, and naval stores. The tree is now endangered due to clear-cutting throughout this time period.

The First Presbyterian Church of Prattville began in 1846 with 13 members and W. H. Mitchell as founding minister, in a building later moved from Bridge to Sixth Street. Poet Sidney Lanier once served as the organist. A second church was built at the original location in 1896 and was expanded several times before it burned in 1941. It was rebuilt the same year and was also added to over the years, until a new sanctuary was completed in 2008.

PRESBYTERIAN CHURCH, PRATTVILLE, ALA.

30344

My home's in Alabama, No matter where I lay my head. My home's in Alabama, Southern born and Southern bred.

— NEIL MORET (lyrics to "My Home's in Alabama")

Continental Gin Co., Prattville, Ala.

In 1838, Daniel Pratt bought 2,000 acres in Autauga County to build a New England-style mill town. His "gin shop" employed some 175 men who produced some 1,500 gins a year for the worldwide cotton trade. Later known as Continental Eagle Company, it survived into the 20th century.

109

Prattville Cotton Mills and Pond, Prattville, Ala.

21705-C

To provide power for his factory, Daniel Pratt dammed Autauga Creek, thus creating the pond shown here. Across the pond are cotton mills and other buildings erected as Prattville grew into a thriving town.

The Bibb Graves Bridge is a rainbow arch bridge that spans the Coosa River in Wetumpka. It is named for Bibb Graves, the 38th governor of Alabama and the first Alabama governor to serve two four-year terms. It is said to be one of only two U.S. bridges with reinforced concrete arches.

BIBB GRAVES BRIDGE, NAMED IN HONOR OF THE GOVERNOR OF ALABAMA—4

110

Originally known as the Alabama State Penitentiary, Wetumpka State opened as the first prison in Alabama in 1842. Its nickname was "The Walls of Alabama," or "Walls." Wetumpka State Prison became a women's prison in 1922; in 1941 it was renamed Julia Tutwiler State Women's Prison.

In the Walls of Penitentiary, Wetumpka, Ala.

The Mills, looking west, Tallassee, Ala.

Tallassee had cotton and woolen mills as early as 1841, located to take advantage of the water power of the Tallassee Falls on the Tallapoosa River. The second mill in Alabama to be run on water power was located in Tallassee. The mills were in operation for 160 years.

Miller Hotel
Dadeville, Alabama

The Miller Hotel was constructed in 1923. It closed in the 1950s and the building is now part of the Dadeville Historic District.

A revival on Herzfeld Hill in 1872 resulted in the start of two of Alexander City's earliest churches, First Baptist, shown here, and First United Methodist. First Baptist Church's first house-of-worship was built in 1877, and the church erected new sanctuaries on the same site in 1906 and in 1967.

Tallapoosa County attracted thousands of miners. The Hillabee mine, also known as the Hog Mountain mine, was operated by the Hillabee Gold Mining Company in 1890. In 1936, production at the mine led Alabama to be recognized as the top producer in the Appalachian states

These houses belonged to some of the leading citizens of Tuskegee. They display architecture typical of the late 1900s—some of them the white-columned Old South style, some with the Queen Anne details popular in the 1890s, and some tending to the traditional red-brick Georgian style.

113

No. 3396.   Rockefeller Square, Tuskegee Institute, Tuskegee, Ala.

Copyright 1907, by A. L. Bedou. New Orleans.

Photograph of Rockefeller Square at the perimeter of Tuskegee's campus in 1907, taken by Arthur Bedou. The photograph shows the Collis P. Huntington Memorial Building, completed in 1906. Collis P. Huntington Hall was designed by Robert R. Taylor, the first African American graduate of MIT.

White Hall, Girls' Dormitory, Tuskegee Institute, Alabama

6A585N

White Hall was constructed in 1910 under the architectural guidance of Robert R. Taylor. It was forced to close due to severe weather damage in 1996 but reopened after a multi-million dollar restoration campaign. It is still in use as an honors dormitory.

114

Dorothy Hall was built in 1901, donated by Olivia and Caroline Phelps Stokes in memory of their great-great-great-grandmother. It was designed by Tuskegee architecture professor Robert R. Taylor. In its early years it was used for industrial training for girls.

Dorothy Hall, Tuskegee Institute, Alabama

9A507-N

THE JOHN A. ANDREW MEMORIAL HOSPITAL, OPEN FOR THE ACCOMMODATION OF COLORED PATIENTS.

Founded in 1913 and named after abolitionist John Albion Andrew, the John A. Andrew Hospital was one of the first hospitals in the country to provide treatment for African American patients and employment for African American medical personnel.

115

Milbank Agricultural Building, Tuskegee Institute, Ala.

1B156-N

Milbank Agricultural Building was one of the Tuskegee buildings designed by Robert R. Taylor, who was recruited to Tuskegee by Booker T. Washington. Taylor spent most of his career at Tuskegee as college architect and director of mechanical industries.

*Union Springs
Presbyterian Church,
at 203 E. Hardaway
St., was organized
in 1853. The present
church was erected
in 1883 and is said to
have been designed
by a Philadelphia
architect..*

116

*Union Springs was
settled in the early
1830s and officially
incorporated in
1844. Bullock County
Courthouse is on the
left, with matching
twin towers.
The Confederate
Monument seen
in the middle of
the street was
later moved to
the Confederate
Cemetery.*

VILLULA TEA GARDEN
SEALE, ALA.

*Villula Tea Garden
was a restaurant and
gift shop operated
from the late 1940s
to the 1970s by
Mrs. Helen Joerg
in Seale, a small
community in Russell
County. Because of
its location near the
military reservation
at Fort Benning,
Georgia, it received
visitors from far-
flung places.*

Denson Boulevard
U. S. Highway 29 Entering Fairfax, Ala.

*Completion of
Interstates 65 and 85
in the 1970s turned
once-bustling U.S.
Highway 29 into a
less-traveled road.
Still, it connects
numerous smaller
towns and cities and
passes by Auburn
University, Troy
University, and
Tuskegee University.
Fairfax is in
Chambers County.*

117

FIRST METHODIST CHURCH, LANETT, ALA.

The First Methodist Church of Lanett, in Chambers County, was organized in 1895. This building was erected in 1915, and members were extremely proud that all debt for the building was cleared by 1918. It was replaced in 1966.

Lanett is a portmanteau of the town's two major textile industrialists: Lafayette Lanier and Theodore Bennett. Lanett Bleachery and Dye Works opened in 1985 and consolidated wih the West Point Manufacturing Company in West Point, Georgia, in 1956.

The Lanett Bleachery and Dye Works
Lanett, Ala.

BB500-N

Chambers County Court House, Lafayette, Ala.

1462-29

The Chambers County Courthouse in LaFayette was built in 1899 and is in use today virtually unaltered. It stands in the middle of a traditional market square in the center of town. It is built of red brick with white masonry trim.

119

Methodist Church, La Fayette, Ala.

The First United Methodist Church of LaFayette was constructed in 1914–15. The Gothic building cost $22,000 ($520,000 today). Located at 104 N. LaFayette Street, the building is still in use.

STREET SCENE, WEDOWEE, ALA.

Pub. by Parker Drug Store.

2087

Wedowee is the county seat of Randolph County, located in the Appalachian foothills, in eastern central Alabama, on the Georgia border. The county was created in 1832, and Wedowee became the county seat in 1835.

Montevallo in Shelby County was founded as Wilson's Hill in the early 1820s on the banks of Shoal Creek. The name was changed in 1826 in a futile effort to make the community more appealing as a possible site for the University of Alabama. Wilson's Hill was founded near a major spring, one of several in the vicinity.

A SCENE AT THE SPRING, MONTEVALLO, ALA.

Published by Chisholm Bros., Portland, Me,

JEFFERSON COUNTY

TERMINAL STATION AND SUBWAY

James Powell, one of the founders of Birmingham, was the first to call Birmingham "the magic city." In his 1873 report to his stockholders, he praised Birmingham as "this little magic city of ours." The sign was built in 1926 as a gift from E. M. Elliott and originally read "Welcome to Birmingham: The Magic City."

YOU'RE LOOKING FOR A PLACE, YOU SAY,
WHERE LUCK IS NEVER DOWN—
JUST PACK YOUR GRIP AND STEP THIS WAY
FOR BIRMINGHAM'S THE TOWN.

Postcards were often used as an advertising medium, for a locale as well as for an individual business. Businesses often joined together in campaigns to attract attention to their town. This postcard encouraging travel to Birmingham is from the 1910s.

THE OLD MILL, MOUNTAIN BROOK ESTATE, BIRMINGHAM, ALA.—26

John Perryman built a grist mill in Mountain Brook at the end of the Civil War; it closed in 1887 but in 1927 developer Robert Jemison built a William H. Kessler-designed replica on the same spot, hoping to create a gathering place for the community.

122

FIRST BAPTIST CHURCH, CORNER 6TH AVE. AND 22ND STREET, NORTH, BIRMINGHAM, ALA.

The First Baptist Church of Birmingham was formed in 1872, and this, its third church building, was built in 1903. During the civil rights movement the congregation voted to receive visitors of all races. In 1984 the church moved to a new location, and the church pictured here was demolished.

The 16-story Empire Building, located at 1928 1st Ave. North in Birmingham, was built in 1909, the tallest building in the state when it opened. It was built by Robert Jemison's Empire Improvement Company, designed by local architects William T. Warren and William Leslie Welton, working with J.E.R. Carpenter of New York. On January 30, 1917, Harry "The Human Fly" Gardiner climbed to the top while thousands of people watched.

123

There is nothing of vanished glory about Birmingham. It is like no other Alabama town. . . . The rhythm of living is quick. The air is alive with the catch-phrases of industrialism.

— CARL CARMER, *Stars Fell on Alabama*, 1934

St. Vincent's Hospital, Birmingham, Ala.

St. Vincent's Hospital was founded in 1898 by Father Patrick O'Reilly and the Daughters of Charity of St. Vincent's DePaul. The first building they constructed, shown here, was formally dedicated on November 29, 1900. It was designed by Thomas Walter III.

124

Howard College was founded by the Alabama chapter of the Southern Baptist Convention; it opened in Marion in 1841. It moved to the East Lake section of Birmingham in 1887 with 157 students enrolled. The central focus of the campus was "Old Main," the large building in the upper center of the picture.

The Phoenix Club, South Highlands, Birmingham, Ala.

The Phoenix Club, organized in April 1883, was for Jewish gentlemen. In 1898 it was re-incorporated by the Alabama Legislature on terms that gave the club the right to provide its members with alcohol, tobacco, and pool tables. In 1909, the club opened at 20th Street and 15th Avenue.

125

11192. Italian Gardens of Mr. Richard W. Massey, Birmingham, Ala.

The Richard Massey mansion was built in 1904 by Joseph Clifford Turner. After it was sold to Massey, he made the gardens into the showplace of Birmingham, hiring an Italian gardener to design a park filled with aromatic plants and imported statuary. Many parties, dances, and weddings were held here.

This postcard is an oddity, because it depicts a pose and configuration of the actual cast-iron statue—the world's largest—that never existed. "The Vulcan" by Guiseppe Moretti stands atop Red Mountain overlooking downtown Birmingham (and famously mooning the suburb of Homewood to the south). Created as Birmingham's entry for the 1904 World's Fair, the likeness of the Roman god of the forge stands 56 feet tall.

126

Vulcan was not the most beautiful statue at the St. Louis Exposition, but he was the biggest and the most talked about.

— KATHRYN TUCKER WINDHAM, *One Big Front Porch,* 2007

View at Five Points, showing Monument of the Beloved Reverend Brother, J. A. Bryan, Birmingham, Ala.

35

The statue of James Alexander Bryan, known as Brother Bryan, was dedicated in 1934 at Five Points South in Birmingham. Brother Bryan was known for his efforts to help the poor and homeless, as well as for his support for civil rights. His statue remains a Birmingham landmark.

127

Jefferson County Court House and Library, Birmingham, Alabama

The construction of the Jefferson County Courthouse and Library, built using reinforced concrete, granite, and limestone, was completed in 1931. The North Annex was built in 1964.

Turning coal into coke was an important step in the iron and steel industry that fueled Birmingham's growth in the late 19th and early 20th centuries. Coal mined in the area was baked into coke, and transported by rail into Birmingham to the iron and steel mills.

128

The Ensley Furnace operated from 1888 to 1976 and was for many years the largest producer of steel and rail in the South. It was funded through a joint investment by Enoch Ensley and the Tennessee Coal, Iron, and Railroad Company. Today the site is under consideration for redevelopment as an industrial park.

Due to Morris Avenue's close proximity to railroad depots, it became Birmingham's commercial and warehouse district early in the city's history. It is named after Josiah Morris, one of the shareholders of the Elyton Land Company who founded Birmingham.

129

The first Methodist church of Birmingham— then a part of the Methodist Episcopal Church South— was organized in June 1872. The congregation built its third building, pictured here, in 1892, designed by noted church architect George Kramer of Ohio.

B-42—Comer Building, Birmingham, Ala.

The Comer Building was built in 1913 and was designed by William C. Weston. It is 27 stories tall and was the tallest skyscraper in Alabama until 1969. Constructing this building was extremely expensive; when the first tenant, the Jefferson County Savings Bank, failed in 1915, some blamed it on the cost of the building.

130

Birmingham is not like the rest of the state. It is an industrial monster sprung up in the midst of a slow-moving pastoral. . . . Birmingham is a new city in an old land.

— CARL CARMER, *Stars Fell on Alabama*, 1934

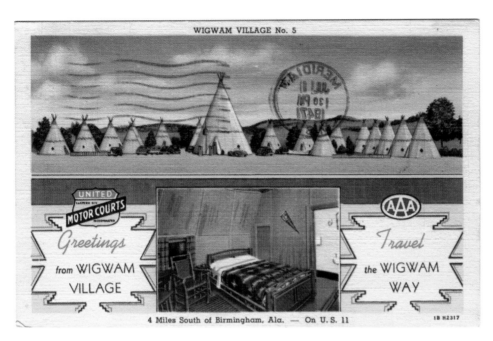

WIGWAM VILLAGE No. 5

UNITED MOTOR COURTS
Greetings from WIGWAM VILLAGE

Travel the WIGWAM WAY

AAA

4 Miles South of Birmingham, Ala. — On U.S. 11

1B H2317

Wigwam Village No. 5 opened in 1941. It was part of a chain of seven motels devised by Frank Redford of Kentucky. The Bessmer Wigwam (No. 5 of the 7) consisted of 15 wigwams in a semicircle, with three more in the center, one containing a restaurant, and two smaller ones for offices.

131

LEGION FIELD STADIUM

Construction on Legion Field began in 1926 and was completed in 1927 as a 21,000-seat stadium. It was named for the American Legion, and bronze plaques inscribed with the names of American soldiers who died in World War I were installed on the towers at the formal entrance.

Originally called the Southside Grammar School, the Paul Hayne School was built in 1886, with the four-story addition on the right added in 1889. The name honored South Carolina poet Paul Hamilton Hayne, who took a personal interest in the school.

132

East Lake Park was developed in 1886 on a 45-acre lake for the East Lake Land company. By 1923, the park had served as home to a ferris wheel, a shooting gallery, a golf course, multiple amusement park style rides, and more. Today, it remains one of the largest municipal recreational facilities in the state.

Founded in 1874 as the Free School, this was the first school in Birmingham. It was later renamed in honor of James Powell, a founder and early mayor of Birmingham. The school was closed in 2001, and the building was badly damaged by fire in 2011, but efforts are being made to save it.

133

Highlands United Methodist Church, originally Five Points Methodist Episcopal, was begun in 1904 by four women who called for a Methodist Sunday School in the Five Points neighborhood. The sanctuary was completed in 1909, and the bells were added in 1921.

The M. Paul
Phillips Library
at Birmingham-
Southern was
dedicated on
November 23, 1923.
It was named for
M. Paul Phillips,
a Birmingham
businessman who
had donated $50,00
for the construction
of the new library.
It served as the
College's Library for
fifty years.

LIBRARY, BIRMINGHAM SOUTHERN COLLEGE, BIRMINGHAM, ALA.—19

134

Vestavia was a
twenty-acre estate
completed by
George B. Ward in
1929. Ward built a
mansion modeled
after the Temple of
Vesta in Rome as
well as gardens and a
gazebo. When Ward
died in 1940, he
originally meant for
the gazebo to serve
as his mausoleum,
but city laws did not
allow it.

VESTAVIA, THE COUNTRY HOME OF MR. GEO. B. WARD, CREST OF SHADES MOUNTAIN, BIRMINGHAM, ALA.

110585

"CASCADE PLUNGE," 68TH ST. AND 2ND AVE. SOUTH, BIRMINGHAM, ALA.

Cascade Plunge opened as a large private swimming pool around 1925 and remained in use into the 1970s. The pool, the largest in the area, was fed by a natural spring. The Cloud Room, a ballroom used for dances and other events, was also part of the facility. The property was recently put up for sale.

135

HILLMAN HOSPITAL, BIRMINGHAM, ALA.—68

Hillman Hospital opened in 1888 to provide medical care for the poor of any race or gender. It was founded by a group of women incorporated as the Daughters of United Charity; the original hospital was called the Hospital of United Charity. It is Birmingham's oldest hospital.

The 1901 Birmingham City Hall was home to municipal offices, the Fire Department, a National Guard unit, the Birmingham Public Library, shops, and a gymnasium. After fires in 1925 and 1944, the library and city hall were moved to new locations at Woodrow Wilson Park.

136

The second Jefferson County Courthouse was built in 1889 by Architects Henry Wolters of Louisville and Charles Wheelock of Birmingham. The massive edifice was built of wood and stone in the Richardsonian Romanesque style popular at the time; the 180-foot bell tower became one of the city's landmarks.

The Thomas Jefferson Hotel, at 1631 2nd Avenue North, was completed in 1929. Among its many amenities was a rooftop mooring mast for dirigibles. Many celebrities stayed at the Thomas Jefferson over the years, including Presidents Hoover and Coolidge and entertainers George Burns, Jerry Lee Lewis, Ethel Merman, Ray Charles, and Pete Rose. A special suite was reserved on the 20th floor for University of Alabama coach Paul "Bear" Bryant.

137

Those red shirts pour onto the field, and then, coming behind them, with that inexorable big cat walk of his, the man himself, the Bear.

— Howell Raines, "Goodbye to the Bear," *New Republic,*

January 23, 1983

The Tutwiler was named for Edward Magruder Tutwiler, who invested profit he had received from selling coal mines. Architects were William Lee Stoddard and William Leslie Welton. The Tutwiler was lavishly built at a cost of $1.5 million. It became a social center for the city, a meeting place for the socially and politically prominent. Visitors included President Warren G. Harding, Charles Lindbergh, and Eleanor Roosevelt.

138

Sweet home Alabama, Where the skies are so blue, Sweet home Alabama, Lord I'm coming home to you.

— LYNARD SKYNARD (lyrics to "Sweet Home Alabama")

13—Noble Street, Looking North, Anniston, Ala.

The Cameo Theater, on the left, was built in 1939, with seating for 936. The building operated as a theater until 1955 and was later used for commercial space. On the right side of the street, the three-story brick building with ornamented side windows is the Anniston National Bank.

Hotel
JEFFERSON DAVIS
"COURTEOUS SERVICE"
Anniston, Alabama

ANNISTON'S ONLY FIREPROOF HOTEL, 160 ROOMS, STRICTLY MODERN

When built in 1917, at 1301 Noble Street, this was the Manhattan Hotel; the name was changed around 1926. "Fireproof" in the postcard caption was a nod to the two major hotel fires Anniston suffered in the 20th century.

The U.S. War Department opened Camp McClellan on July 18, 1917 after entering World War I. The camp was organized into clusters of tents; this cluster is designated for the training of machine-gun units. Transportation around the facility could be carried on by rail, as seen on the bottom left corner.

140

Noble Institute for Girls was a private girls' school established in 1886 and funded by Samuel Noble, one of Anniston's founders. The imposing brick and stone building was located at 11th Street and Leighton Avenue, next door to Grace Episcopal Church, which helped to supervise the school.

Night Scene on Noble St. Anniston Ala.

Noble Street, named for the city's founder Samuel Noble, is Anniston's main thoroughfare. Anniston was the first city in Alabama to be lit by electricity; the system was constructed in 1882, and the street lights were first lit in 1912—the first "white way" system in a Southern city.

U. S. NATIONAL GUARD, CAMP MC CLELLAN, ANNISTON, ALA.

KNIGHTS OF COLUMBUS EVERYBODY WELCOME

KNIGHTS OF COLUMBUS BUILDING.

During World War I, the Catholic fraternal service organization Knights of Columbus provided support for troops both in camps in the U.S. and on the battlefields of Europe. One of the Knights' buildings was located at Camp McClellan in Anniston, a training base for National Guard troops.

Samuel Noble Monument, Anniston, Ala.

Samuel Noble (1834–1888) was born in England, and after the Civil War came to eastern Alabama and established the Woodstock Iron Company in 1873. As the company prospered, Noble envisioned building a utopian community around it. He provided education, housing, and benefits to the workers. Anniston became a flourishing community with his leadership and support. At his sudden death in 1888 some 5,000 people attended his funeral.

When Noble visited the area in 1869, "The wild beauty of Choccolocco Valley and the presence of abundant iron ore and other minerals convinced him that an industrial town could be developed here."

— Alabama: A Guide to the Deep South, 1941

14362—Oxford Lake Park, Anniston, Ala.

Oxford Lake Park was established in 1889 as a privately owned amusement park. Located on McCulley's Spring, it advertised recreational activities such as fishing, swimming, and boating, as well as a mini-zoo. In the middle of the lake was "matrimony island," the local lover's lane.

143

Shipping Pig Iron, Anniston, Ala.

Anniston had an iron furnace during the Civil War that was destroyed by Union cavalry in 1865. The Woodstock Iron Company reopened the furnace in 1872 and specialized in manufacturing iron, steel, and pipe clay. Anniston was proud of its foundries; one local newspaper was named the Anniston Hot Blast.

Anniston had two USO clubs: one for white soldiers and one for African Americans. The clubs provided entertainment and recreation to soldiers on leave and those enlisted men waiting to be shipped to bases overseas.

144

Many of the buildings at Fort McClellan, including this post exchange, were built in the 1930s by the Works Progress Administration, or WPA. The buildings were designed in a Spanish Colonial Revival style.

HUTMENTS, FORT MC CLELLAN, ALA.—67

Fort McClellan, named for General George McClellan, was established in 1917 to train troops for WWI. The base was retained after WWI and in 1929 became Fort McClellan. During WWII it was expanded to serve as an artillery training base; half a million soldiers came to Fort McClellan to train.

145

TENT PITCHING CLASS, FORT MC CLELLAN, ANNISTON, ALA.—62

Training at Fort McClellan was conducted in conditions as near as possible to actual combat. Among other units, the 27th Infantry Division of the New York National Guard and the 92nd Infantry Division, a segregated division of African American soldiers, trained at Fort McClellan.

Barber Memorial Seminary was a school for African American girls, funded with a bequest from Margaret A. Barber of Philadelphia. The school opened in 1896, and in 1930 the college division merged with Scotia Women's College of Concord and became Barber-Scotia College.

146

The Anniston Inn Kitchen, built in 1885, originally occupied the Lakeview Hotel. In 1894, the building became home to the Anniston College for Young Ladies. The college disbanded in 1909, and a 1923 fire destroyed the majority of the structure. The remainders of the building now serve as an event center.

STREET SCENE - ANNISTON, ALA.

Anniston loved parades of all types— political parades, labor day parades, homecoming parades, parades honoring soldiers and returning veterans. It is not clear just what this parade was in support of, but it obviously drew a large crowd.

147

EAST SIDE PUBLIC SQUARE, JACKSONVILLE, ALA.

Most of the buildings visible to the right are still standing and in use for commercial purposes. The statue barely visible in the center of the square is a monument to Major General John Horace Forney, a Confederate soldier and local hero. General Forney survived the war and died in 1902.

ANNISTON INN, ANNISTON, ALA.

Anniston Inn was built in 1885 by Samuel Noble, using plans drawn up by the famous architect Stanford White. With handcrafted woodwork and stained glass, and as the first hotel in the U.S. to be lit by incandescent electricity, it was considered the finest hotel in the South.

Now the Anniston Museum of Natural History, the Regar Museum opened in 1930 in the town's Carnegie Library. The Museum's collections began with a bird exhibit created by naturalist William H. Werner, who displayed his collection on the boardwalk in Atlantic City, New Jersey.

Interior, Regar Museum of Natural History, Seventh Largest, Anniston, Ala.

7—Clubhouse of Business and Professional Women's Club Anniston, Ala.

The Business and Professional Women's Club cabin was built in 1936 on Rocky Holly in Anniston. The rustic log cabin was initially a meeting place for Anniston women seeking professional growth. The club disbanded in 1976, and the cabin is currently a part of the Anniston Parks System.

149

ANNISTON COUNTRY CLUB, ANNISTON, ALA.—11

The Anniston Country Club was founded in 1909 and held its formal opening on June 8, 1910. It is still in operation; its facilities, including golf courses and tennis courts, have expanded over the years.

The First Presbyterian Church of Anniston was founded in 1884 as the town was rebuilding from Civil War and Reconstruction. A chapel was dedicated in 1886, and the main structure, with its distinctive pagoda-style tower, was completed a decade later. It was expanded several more times and remained in use until the congregation built a new church in 1963.

ANNISTON, ALA.   First Presbyterian Church.

5229

For human beings conditioned to a set way of life in a demanding land, there were snatches of pleasure in community gatherings, in family associations, in church meetings, and even in the mere matter of neighborliness.

— WADE HALL, *Conecuh People*

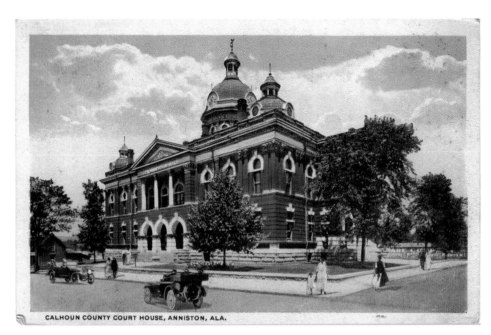

CALHOUN COUNTY COURT HOUSE, ANNISTON, ALA.

The Calhoun County Courthouse, located at the northeast corner of 11th Street and Gurnee in Anniston, was completed in 1900. J. W. Gulucke and Company were architects. On January 15, 1931, the building was gutted by a spectacular fire, watched by a crowd of thousands.

151

THE ALABAMA HOTEL, ANNISTON, ALA.

The Alabama Hotel was located on Noble Street in downtown Anniston. During WWII, visitors to soldiers at nearby Fort McClellan crowded the building. On September 15, 1944, brimming with over 200 guests, the building caught fire. Two people died and the hotel was a total loss.

*Oxford Lake,
built in 1889 on
McCulley's Spring,
was advertised as a
half-hour ride from
Anniston on the
electric car line. The
park was acquired by
the city of Anniston
in 1955 and is still
in operation. It
celebrated its 100th
anniversary on April
15, 1989.*

DRIVEWAY, OXFORD LAKE, ANNISTON, ALA.

152

*The state college
at Jacksonville,
founded in 1883, was
Jacksonville State
Teachers' College
from 1929 until 1957.
This picture shows
the college early in
the teachers' college
period, with three
major buildings:
from left, Hames
Hall, Weatherly Hall,
and Forney Hall.*

State Teachers' College, Jacksonville, Ala.

ETOWAH COUNTY

Looking down the Coosa River from Gadsden—Elliot Peach Orchard in the distance, containing 80,000 bearing trees.

The Elliott Peach Orchard, owned by Capt. James M. Elliott Jr., was a major economic force in the Gadsden area in the 1890s. The orchard was made up of 80,000 trees, and peaches were canned and shipped all over the country. The Gadsden Country Club now sits on the site of the orchard.

153

COUNTRY CLUB, GADSDEN, ALA.—10

The Gadsden Country Club, founded in 1919, was built on land donated by the succeeding president of the First National Bank of Gadsden and founder of Agricola Furnace Company, Otto Agricola. Today the club includes pools, tennis courts, and more.

Located at 600 Broad Street, the Post Office is also known as the Federal Building and Courthouse in Gadsden. It was constructed in 1909 and has been a courthouse, post office, and government office building. The structure was originally one story; the third and fourth floors were added later.

POST OFFICE, GADSDEN, ALA.

104444

The Holy Name of Jesus Hospital was founded in 1926 by the Sisters of the Missionary Servants of the Most Blessed Trinity. The group was a Catholic order that operated out of Opelika in the early 1900s. The tall cross—green for the color of the order—atop the hospital became a Gadsden landmark.

HOLY NAME OF JESUS HOSPITAL, GADSDEN, ALA.—13

DWIGHT COTTON MILLS, ALABAMA CITY, NEAR GADSDEN, ALA.—8

The Dwight Cotton Mills near Gadsden were built in 1894–96 by the Dwight Manufacturing Company. On July 12, 1934, the workers at the Dwight Mills went out on strike; the movement spread across the state and eventually across the entire country—the largest labor conflict in American history.

155

ETOWAH TUBERCULOSIS SANITARIUM ON LOOKOUT MOUNTAIN, NEAR GADSDEN, ALA.—15

It was long believed that fresh air was a beneficial treatment for tuberculosis patients. In 1918 Etowah County established a "fresh air camp" to provide such treatment. When the camp was destroyed by fire in 1926, the Etowah County Tuberculosis Santarium was built.

The First Baptist Church of Gadsden organized in 1855 and met in a wooden building for its first five years. The church shown here is the fourth church building. It was dedicated in November 20, 1927, and remains the home of the congregation.

156

The Gadsden municipal swimming pool was built in the 1940s on South First Street. It was a popular site for swim meets, as local swim clubs gathered to compete. By 1950 several additional pools were built in various locations around the city. The municipal pool was open through 1963.

Emma Sansom Monument, Gadsden, Alabama   116

Silvey Photo

During the Civil War, a Union unit of 1700 troops burned a bridge over the creek near teenager Emma Sansom's home. According to legend and myth, the girl led Confederate General Nathan Bedford Forrest and his 600 troops to a ford where they could safely cross the creek. Forrest was then able to defeat the Union detachment at the Battle of Cedar Bluff, and Emma became a local heroine. The United Daughters of the Confederacy dedicated a statue in her honor on July 4, 1907.

157

In time of war, send me all the Alabamians you can get, but in time of peace, for Lord's sake, send them to someone else.

— General Edward H. Plummer, on the Alabama troops of the Rainbow division, whom he commanded in WWI

Noccalula Falls is a public park in Gadsden. It is marked by a statue of a Cherokee woman, Noccalula, erected in the 1960s. According to legend, the woman plunged to her death over the falls after she was ordered to marry a man she did not love.

158

The Etowah County Courthouse in Gadsden was dedicated on October 25, 1890. It was built of brick, trimmed with blue granite, and featured a lofty 126-foot clock tower. Political candidates often spoke from the front steps. The courthouse was designed by architect John A. Scott.

MADISON COUNTY

20100—Street Scene, HUNTSVILLE, Ala.

The west side of Courthouse Square in Huntsville was known as "Cotton Row," since many cotton brokers had offices on the square and conducted sales negotiations in the street. On Cotton Market Day farmers brought their baled cotton to sell. Mules and wagons are being used to transport the bales in this picture.

The Spring and Ford, Huntsville, Ala.

Big Spring Park was a location sought out by Huntsville's founder John Hunt. For a century and a half, the spring served as the city's water supply. Today, the park houses many gifts from other countries such as the red Japanese bridge and cherry trees given by Japanese Major General Mikio Kimata.

The Elks Building, located at the corner of Green and Eustis, was designed by local architect Edgar L. Love and built in 1905. The theater—sometimes called the opera house—was built with a floor that sloped upward from the street into the theater. It was a popular site for plays, performances and local events.

THE ELKS THEATRE, HUNTSVILLE, ALA.

160

These three houses are not "colonial" in the historical sense; they were built in the early 19th century. All three houses are still standing, and the house labeled "No. 1" is considered the oldest house in Alabama, built in 1814 by Col. Leroy Pope.

H-7—Clement C. Clay Bridge over Tennessee River near Huntsville, Ala.

The Clement C. Clay Bridge opened in 1931. A cantilever truss bridge, it carried two-way traffic on U.S. 231. It was named for Clement Comer Clay, the eighth governor of Alabama, who also served as the first chief justice of the Alabama Supreme court and as a U.S. Senator.

161

THE STATE AGRICULTURAL AND MECHANICAL COLLEGE FOR NEGROES, HUNTSVILLE, ALA.

2A-H853

Now Alabama A&M, the college was originally founded as a State Normal School for African American teachers in 1873. In 1891, it received funds to become a land-grant college and by 1896, the name was changed to the State Agricultural and Mechanical College for Negroes.

The Jupiter-C, left, was developed at the Army Ballistic Missile Agency in Huntsville and used to launch the free-world's first scientific satellite, the Explorer. *The rocket on the right was the U.S. Army's Jupiter, an intermediate range ballistic missile, also developed in Huntsville, but never actually deployed. It would have carried a nuclear warhead as far as 1500 nautical miles. A Jupiter-C is displayed at the U.S. Space and Rocket Center in Huntsville.*

162

When the first earth satellite, Explorer I, was launched, "Huntsville traffic stopped for jubilant celebrations. . . . Yells and fireworks . . . continued late into the night."

— HELEN MORGAN AKENS AND VIRGINIA POUNDS BROWN, *Alabama: Mounds to Missiles*, 1962

First Army Ordnance Guided Missile Ever Placed On Public Display
HERMES RESEARCH TEST MISSILE
REDSTONE ARSENAL · HUNTSVILLE, ALABAMA.

Although Redstone Arsenal is known for the work of the Marshall Space Flight Center, it is also a center for missile command. The Hermes was an early missile series developed at Redstone. Its first showing—"the first army ordnance guided missile ever placed on public display"—took place in 1953.

163

THE WEEDEN HOMESTEAD
HUNTSVILLE, ALABAMA
"BANDANNA BALLADS".

Built in 1819, this house was purchased by Dr. William Weeden in 1845 and occupied by his descendants until 1956, except for a brief period when it was confiscated as quarters for Union troops in the Civil War. Today it is maintained as a museum, located at 300 Gates Avenue in Huntsville.

Maple Grove Cottages.

Huntsville, Ala. U. S. 241 N. 1 mi.

Maple Grove Cottages are now rented as apartments. The complex was also known as the Maple Grove Motel. Maple Grove Cottages advertised, among other modern features, ceiling fans.

This is the second Madison County Courthouse, located at the corner of South Side Square and East Side Square. The building, designed by local architect George Steele, was erected in 1837–40. The dome was copper.

THE COURT HOUSE AND CONFEDERATE MONUMENT, HUNTSVILLE, ALA.

Hotel Twickenham, Huntsville, Ala.—3

The Hotel Twickenham operated between 1915 and 1971. The Twickenham's name came from the first name given to Huntsville; Leroy Pope bought land in the area and laid out a town to be called "Twickenham" after the English estate of his cousin, poet Alexander Pope.

165

H-16—Merrimack Mfg. Co., a Model Cotton Mill and Village, Huntsville, Ala.

The Merrimack Manufacturing Company of Lowell, Massachusetts, built a cotton spinning plant in Huntsville in 1900. At the beginning 60 houses were built to provide residences for workers; over the next few years the mill and the village were expanded several times.

Dallas Mill began operation in Huntsville on November 16, 1892. It manufactured cotton sheeting and by 1900, had doubled in size to meet demand. The Dallas Mill was the largest mill in the area and one of the finest in the South. It had so many employees that an entire suburb emerged around it.

The Dallas Mills, Huntsville, Ala.

Huntsville has grown up around a "big spring" that flows from under a bluff, the largest limestone spring in north Alabama. As early as 1825 the spring was providing water to the town and was the main source of water for the city of Huntsville into the 20th century.

The Big Spring, Huntsville, Ala.

DECATUR, ALA.

BANK STREET, LOOKING NORTH.

Grant St. looking West from Eighth Ave., Albany, Ala.

Bank Street anchors the historic district in Decatur and is named after the state bank that was established in the town in 1832. At the time, Decatur was the only location in the Tennessee Valley where riverboat, wagon, and rail routes converged. The additional presence of the bank helped the town grow into a commercial center.

Albany was founded in 1887 as New Decatur. At its conception, the original streets bore the names of two Federal and two Confederate generals so as to appeal to both Northern and Southern settlers. These were Grant and Sherman Streets and Johnston and Jackson Streets, respectively.

Named after early settler George Hartselle, Hartselle developed along the L&N Railroad. The town was the center of cotton-ginning in Morgan County. Note that the crops— cotton on the right, possibly sorghum cane on the left— grow right up to the edge of the road. Not an inch of ground is wasted.

Highway, North, Hartselle, Ala.

The Morgan County Courthouse was built in 1894 by the architectural firm W. Chamberlain & Co. It was destroyed by fire in 1926.

Morgan County Court House, Decatur, Ala.

Loading Cotton, Tennessee River, New Decatur, Ala.

New Decatur was founded in 1887 after most of Decatur was burned during the Civil War. Both Decatur and New Decatur relied on their position on the Tennessee River for commerce, and together the two towns formed a center for shipping and travel between Nashville and Mobile.

169

The Crescent Motel, located on U. S. Highway 31 in Decatur, was billed as "The South's Most Glamorous Resort Motel." It offered amenities such as an oval swimming pool and a golf course. It was designed in the streamlined "space-age" style popular in the late 1950s.

Leila Cantwell Seton Hall, Decatur, Ala.

6A630-N

The Old State Bank of Alabama, established in 1830, had three branches; the building in this picture was erected in Decatur for the Tennessee Valley Branch. Over the next century the building was used for several purposes, including a hospital and a residence, as well as a bank.

170

West Main Street, Hartselle, Ala.

Downtown Hartselle experienced major fires in 1901 and 1916. After the 1916 fire, only nine brick buildings remained from the original town. However, many of the buildings that were built after the fires remain today.

TUSCUMBIA, ALA. — LOOKING SOUTH FROM COURT HOUSE.

COPYRIGHT, 1907, BY RAMPSON & CO.

The Colbert County Courthouse is located on North Main Street, and this card shows the view down South Main Street. Most of the business are not identifiable, but to the far left can be seen the public school building. The building with a bell and a Coca-Cola sign is unexpectedly a firehouse.

NITRATE PLANT, NO. 1, MUSCLE SHOALS, ALA.

© BY G. W. LANDRUM.

In 1918, President Woodrow Wilson ordered the construction of the Wilson Dam in Muscle Shoals to provide electricity for two nitrate plants. The nitrate plants were intended to manufacture the supplies necessary for explosives and ammunition for World War I.

171

WILSON DAM POWER HOUSE, MUSCLE SHOALS, ALA.

2A-H881

Wilson Dam was completed in 1924 and cost approximately $47 million to build. After the end of WWI, the Tennessee Valley Authority eventually was established to use the dam, powerhouse, and the plants for development of the area.

172

PERMANENT POWER PLANT, MUSCLE SHOALS, ALA.

© BY G. W. LANDRUM.

The permanent power plant harnesses the power of the Tennessee River as it passes over Wilson Dam and converts it for use as electricity.

SHEFFIELD HOTEL, SHEFFIELD, ALA., IN THE HEART OF THE MUSCLE SHOALS DISTRICT. 58757

The Sheffield Hotel was built in 1890 and was known for its central staircase and chandelier. In the 1930s it was one of the only places in the area where locals could purchase alcohol. In June 1948, it burned to the ground after a fire began on its top floor.

173

TENNESSEE RIVER BRIDGE, SHEFFIELD, ALA.

This bridge was built in 1840 and was the first river bridge in the state. The original structure was a single-deck covered bridge, which was rebuilt in 1858 as a double-deck, with trains using the top deck and vehicles and pedestrians the lower deck. It was burned in the Civil War and rebuilt in 1870.

Wilson Dam not only provides hydroelectric power, but also helps make for a more navigable section of the river. Shoal Creek, originally called the Sycamore River, rises in north Lawrence County, Tennessee, and flows for almost 60 miles before it joins the Tennessee River in Lauderdale County, Alabama.

SHOALS CREEK—CREATED BY THE BACKWATERS OF WILSON DAM, MUSCLE SHOALS, ALA. 2530-29

174

Spring Park, located near the Tuscumbia business district, has been a popular recreational area for many years. Built around a spring-fed lake, it includes an elaborate fountain and one of the world's largest man-made waterfalls.

SPRING PARK, TUSCUMBIA, ALA.

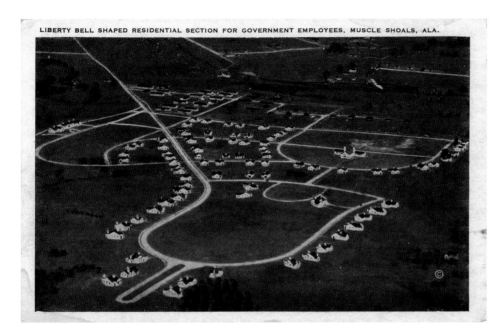

LIBERTY BELL SHAPED RESIDENTIAL SECTION FOR GOVERNMENT EMPLOYEES, MUSCLE SHOALS, ALA.

Eighteen thousand workers were hired to work on construction of the Wilson Dam; a town was built to house the workers, including houses, a hospital, a school, and three barber shops. Pictured here is "Village One," constructed for the workers in Plant 1. The neighborhood was laid out in a liberty bell shape.

175

Birthplace of Helen Keller, Tuscumbia, Ala.

69436-N

One of Alabama's most famous citizens, Helen Keller, was born at Ivy Green in Tuscumbia in 1880. Ivy Green was built in 1820 by Helen Keller's grandparents; she lived in the main house until she was eight years old and later moved to Boston, but she always considered Ivy Green her home.

Big Spring, Tuscumbia, Ala.

The Big Spring sits at the heart of Tuscumbia and provided the town's water supply for its earliest settlements. The town was originally referred to as the Big Spring Community when it was laid out in 1819 but the name was changed to Tuscumbia in 1822.

176

Andrew Jackson formally recommended that a town be established at the point where the Military Road crossed the Tennessee River. The Secretary of War designated the site for the future town, which was finally incorporated in 1885 as the City of Sheffield.

Cliff Scene on Tennessee River, Sheffield, Ala.

FLORENCE, ALA.
City of Beautiful Churches

POPLAR STREET
CHURCH OF CHRIST

FIRST PRESBYTERIAN CHURCH

TRINITY
CHURCH
EPISCOPAL

FIRST METHODIST CHURCH

FIRST BAPTIST
CHURCH

© CURT TEICH & CO., Inc.

Florence University for Women.

The First Presbyterian Church of Florence was established in 1818 and was the first organized church in the town. The Church of Christ started in 1886 as a meeting at the home of Susan Thrasher. The First Baptist Church was built in 1890. Also shown are First Methodist Church and Trinity Church Episcopal.

Florence University for Women began as Baptist University and Hawthorne's College. The college was intended to be a Baptist university, but the school was unable to raise a $100,000 endowment, so it instead opened in 1891 as a secular institution known as Southern Female University.

177

Forks of Cypress was built in the 1830s by James Jackson, one of the founders of Florence, and his wife, Sally Moore Jackson. The house was designed by architect William Nichols, who also designed the Old Alabama State Capitol and the original campus of the University of Alabama.

The Forks of Cypress
Florence, Alabama

Towards the top of the card, the light yellow building is Wesleyan Hall, built in 1856. It was occupied by Union and Confederate troops at different times during the Civil War; General William Tecumseh Sherman is reported to have originated the expression "War is Hell" in Wesleyan Hall.

Aerial View of State Teachers College, Founded 1855, Florence, Ala.

Eliza Coffee Memorial Hospital, Florence, Alabama

The Eliza Coffee Memorial Hospital opened in 1919 in response to the need for acute care in northwest Alabama. The hospital was named for Eliza Croom Coffee, daughter of Captain Alexander Coffee, civic and business leader in Florence, and his second wife Eliza Sloss Coffee.

179

Hotel Reeder, Florence, Ala.

The Hotel Reeder, located on the south side of East Tennessee Street, was one of the most prestigious hotels in Florence in the 1920s. When President Franklin D. Roosevelt visited the area in 1933 to inspect the dam construction, his staff was housed at the Reeder.

East View of Wilson Dam, Muscle Shoals, Florence, Sheffield and Tuscumbia

The Wilson Dam is one of nine Tennessee Valley Authority dams on the Tennessee River. The dam predates the TVA but came under its authority in the 1930s. It is capable of generating 663 megawatts of electricity.

Construction on the Justice John McKinley Federal Building and Post Office began in 1911 and was completed in 1913. The post office filled the first floor while the court and offices occupied the second and third floors. The building was named in 1999 for Justice John McKinley, one of the original founders of Florence.

ELKS' CLUB AND POST OFFICE FROM CITY PARK, FLORENCE, ALA.

65275

First Boat Passing Through 3rd Lock Chamber, Florence, Ala.—10

The Wilson Navigation Lock is one of ten locks that allows for shipping up the Tennessee River. The original lock was finished in 1927 and was upgraded in 1959. At the time of construction, the Wilson Dam and its lock established two world records for damn length and lock lift height.

181

COURT STREET LOOKING NORTH, FLORENCE, ALA.

Court Street, the main street of the Florence business district, is still host to busy stores and restaurants. The entire district was placed on the National Register of Historic Places in 1995.

Joseph Milner and Son was a drugstore that is still in operation today as Milner-Rushing Drugs. The hand-colored card refers to Bluewater Creek. At Dutch Landing in the summers, Bluewater Creek was shallow enough that settlers could easily ford it.

Located near the bank of the Tennessee River, the Florence Indian Mound, otherwise known as "Wawmanona," is 43 feet high and dates back to 500 A.D. The Tennessee Valley's largest domiciliary mound, it was used for ceremonies of Native Americans who lived in the area before the Cherokees and Creeks.

EAST SIDE OF SQUARE.
ATHENS, ALA.

This picture depicts Athens in the early 1900s—before the automobile. A street market for cotton seems to be going on. Some of the buildings are recognizable; the Martin-Richardson-Malone Building, home of the Martin-Richardson Cash Store, still stands today.

183

ATHENS COLLEGE, ATHENS, ALA.

61983-C

The present-day Athens State University began as Athens Female Academy, a private school for girls founded in Athens in 1822. It became a Methodist school in 1842, and a state institution in 1975.

Limestone County Court House, Athens, Ala.

The 1919 courthouse is the fifth to be built in the city of Athens. The architect was Ben Price, who also designed the Highlands United Methodist Church in Birmingham. The courthouse is still being used today with only minor renovations.

184

President Garfield Preached Here

In 1862, local members of the Disciples of Christ invited Garfield, the Union general, to preach at the Mooresville Church. Garfield was one of the few leaders of the denomination who supported the war, since many refused to engage in fighting other church members.

City School Building, Cullman, Ala.

Cullman City Schools was established as a separate district in 1884. This building, constructed in 1909 as Cullman High School, was built by W. A. Schlosser. A second building was added as the enrollment increased, and the building in the picture was used for the elementary grades.

185

The St. Bernard College Campus, St. Bernard, Alabama

Founded in 1929, St. Bernard College was originally established as a junior college. In the 1940s and 1950s, it expanded into a four-year institution with its first class graduating in 1955. It closed in 1979, though the campus is still used by the St. Bernard Preparatory School.

Cotton Scene, Cullman, Ala.

Into the 20th century, cotton was king of Alabama agriculture. Cullman had eight cotton gins. Although the land in Cullman was originally thought unfit for growing cotton, the county went on to produce more cotton than any other county in the state.

The second Cullman County courthouse, built in 1913, replaced an earlier courthouse which was destroyed by fire in 1912. The Cullman Courthouse hosts a shape-note singing every July that dates back to the 1880s, the last of the courthouse singings that were once widespread in Alabama.

Court House, Cullman, Alabama   47822-N

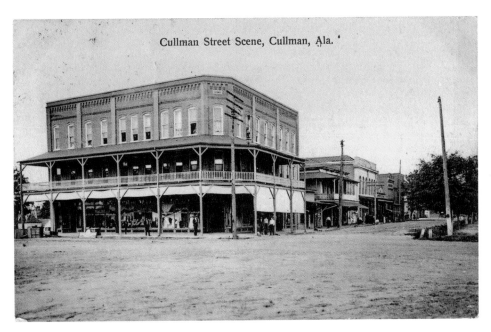

Cullman Street Scene, Cullman, Ala.

Located at First and Fourth streets in downtown Cullman, this building was purchased by E. C. Kinney in 1909. In this picture the first floor is used by a clothing store; over the years the Eureka Hotel and a Rexall Drugstore were among the businesses which also operated in the building.

187

Modern Shrines and Missions, Closer View Facing South, St. Bernard College

The Ave Maria Grotto was designed and built by Brother Joseph Zoettl, a Benedictine Monk at St. Bernard Abbey. The four-acre grotto includes 125 miniature reproductions of religious and secular buildings. This part of the Grotto includes miniature versions of "modern missions," and in the center is the Alamo.

In 1889, Alabama began to establish agricultural schools throughout the state in places like Athens, Hamilton, and Sylacauga. In 1919, the state established a department of vocational agriculture at these schools, and each location became a State Secondary Agricultural School.

State Secondary Agricultural School, Hamilton, Ala.

188

Hamilton was named in honor of Captain A. J. Hamilton's donation of 40 acres of land to the community in 1883. The city of Hamilton's Military Road, shown here, was a road carved by order of Andrew Jackson to create a shorter route between New Orleans and Nashville in 1815.

Military Street Looking South, Hamilton, Ala.

Senator J. H. Bankhead's Residence, Jasper, Ala.

This house was built for Senator John Hollis Bankhead and his wife Tallulah Brockman Bankhead in 1910. The actress Tallulah Bankhead, Senator Bankhead's granddaughter, spent much of her childhood here; she was raised by her grandparents after the death of her mother shortly after her birth.

FRONT STREET LOOKING WEST, CARBON HILL, ALA

Carbon Hill is a small town in western Walker County, near Jasper, and is located on one of the richest deposits of coal in the state. The building on the right is the commissary of the Great Elk Company, a coal company owned by H. S. Jenkins and F. I. Jenkins of Baltimore, Maryland.

189

Musgrove Country Club, Jasper, Ala.

The log building of the Musgrove Country Club was completed in 1924 and is still in use, remodeled and expanded but retaining some of its original features. It was built by Col. L. B. Musgrove as a place to entertain his friends and business associates.

Jasper was settled in 1815 and is named after Sergeant William Jasper, a soldier in the American Revolution. Third Avenue runs through the Jasper Downtown Historic District, a 400-acre section that preserves buildings from the late-19th and early-20th centuries.

Third Avenue, Jasper, Ala.

LOOKING TOWARDS
RED SULPHUR SPRING
—
ST. CLAIR SPRINGS,
ALA.

St. Clair Springs, in St. Clair County, is a "spring yard" made up of seven mineral springs, including the red sulphur spring pictured here. In the late 19th century the area was a popular resort, with a central hotel, boarding houses, and summer homes.

191

The ladies would gather at their favorite springs, sit on the shady benches, and alternately drink water, do fancy work and chat. After luncheon they would rest, then late in the afternoon gather at the springs again.

— JAMES F. SULZBY JR., *Historic Alabama Hotels and Resorts*

Blountsville, incorporated in 1827, is located in Blount County in north central Alabama. Fred's Motel was located on U.S. 231, a major north-south artery that passes through Blountsville. The motel was owned by Mr. and Mrs. Fred Allbritten.

Round the Clock was a 24-hour gas station and cafe on U.S. Highway 231. It was located outside Oneonta and was popular with tourists. Round the Clock sold Pan-Am Gasoline, a brand that was used in the southeast until 1956, when it was rebranded as Amoco.

Prospecting for gold on the Tallapoosa River, near Fruithurst, Alabama, with a No. 3 Traction Machine, owned by Mr. Ray Hubbs.

Fruithurst is a small town in Cleburne County, on the eastern edge of the state. Ray Hubbs was a native of Wisconsin who moved to Alabama; he is listed in census records as a farmer but evidently had an interest in mining as well.

193

Where thy snow white cotton shines, To the hills where coal and iron, Hide in thy exhaustless mines, Strong-armed miners, sturdy farmers, Loyal hearts whate'er we be, Alabama, Alabama, We will aye be true to thee.

— Julia Tutwiler (lyrics to "Alabama," the state song)

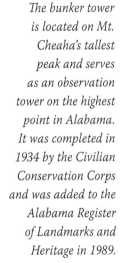

The bunker tower is located on Mt. Cheaha's tallest peak and serves as an observation tower on the highest point in Alabama. It was completed in 1934 by the Civilian Conservation Corps and was added to the Alabama Register of Landmarks and Heritage in 1989.

My mother and father were born in the most beautiful place on earth, in the foothills of the Appalachians along the Alabama-Georgia line. It was a place where gray mists hid the tops of low, deep-green mountains.

— RICK BRAGG, *All Over but the Shoutin'*, 1977

PULPIT ROCK, CHEAHA STATE PARK, ALABAMA—8

Pulpit Rock is a quartzite rock cliff with dramatic views of the country surrounding Mount Cheaha, the highest point in the state. It is popular with hikers and climbers. Mount Cheaha is located in Cheaha State Park, the oldest continuously operating state park in Alabama.

Good Auto Roads. Altitude 1,500 feet. Always Cool.
Aeroplane View of Borden-Wheeler Springs Hotel and Summer Cottage Colony,
Borden Springs, Ala.
One of the best known Summer Resorts in the South.
Midway between Atlanta and Birmingham, on S. A. L. R. R.

Uncle Tom's Cabin.

Wheeler Cottage.

Big Terrapin Creek.

Golf Links.

Hotel.   Dance Pavilion.   Mineral Spring.   Swimming Pool.

195

Located in Cleburne County near the Georgia state line, Borden Springs is surrounded by the foothills of the Appalachian Mountains. The first hotel at Borden Springs was a small 20-room building which had been moved from a spot some 16 miles away.

Cherokee County High School, Centre, Ala.

Cherokee County High School was built in 1908 of bricks that were made on the school grounds. It opened on September 26, 1908, with 49 students. It fielded its first football team in 1920 and had its first undefeated/untied season in 1925.

196

The Mentone Springs Hotel was built in 1884 by Frank Caldwell. The name, meaning "a musical mountain spring," was inspired by a place Queen Victoria traveled to in France. The Mentone Springs Hotel operated for 130 years and was one of the oldest hotels in Alabama until it was destroyed by fire in March 2014.

MENTONE SPRINGS HOTEL
MENTONE, ALA.

Little River on Lookout Mt., near Ft. Payne

Little River runs the length of Lookout Mountain and flows through a canyon into Weiss Lake. The river is home to three waterfalls that have drawn tourists and industry since the area's earliest settlements. In 1992, Congress named the region a national preserve.

197

BETHUNE'S MOTOR COURT, U.S. 11 — ALA. 35, FORT PAYNE, ALA.

Bethune's Motor Court, on U.S. 11 in Fort Payne, was owned and operated by Mr. and Mrs. C. L. Clayton. It advertised up-to-date comforts such as tile baths and hot water heat. It was a 10-minute drive from the motel to DeSoto State Park.

Guntersville Boat Races, Guntersville, Alabama

In 1939, the first boat race on Guntersville Lake was held in celebration of the completion of the Guntersville Dam. A crowd of over 60,000 attended the first races—the largest crowd ever assembled in north Alabama up to that time.

198

Guntersville Dam forms Lake Guntersville, the largest lake in Alabama and the second-largest in the TVA system. It stretches 75 miles from Nickajack Lake in southeast Tennessee to Guntersville Dam, with 949 miles of shoreline.

Guntersville Dam
T. V. A. Dam near Guntersville, Alabama

The J. H. Snead Seminary, Boaz, Ala.

The Boaz Seminary was established by the Methodist Episcopal Church in 1898 and formally opened in 1899 with 70 students. In 1906 the name was changed to honor a local businessman and donor. It became part of Snead State College, a junior college run by the North Alabama Methodist Conference in 1935.

199

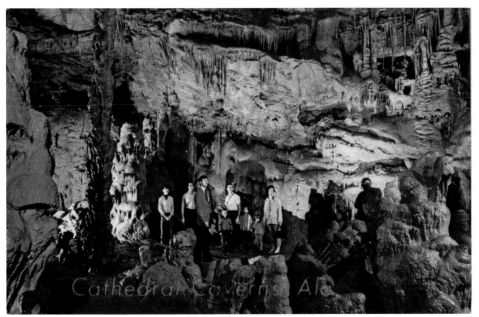

Cathedral Caverns, Ala.

Located in Marshall County, these spectacular limestone caverns formed 320–350 million years ago. From 1955 to 1974, Cathedral Caverns was operated as a private attraction by local entrepreneur Jay Gurley. In May 2000 the site became Cathedral Caverns State Park.

The Kate Duncan Smith School in Grant, Marshall County, is a K-12 school jointly supported by the Daughters of the American Revolution and the Marshall County Board of Education. The school was built with the help of local residents and opened in 1926. Today it is a public school.

200

The George Houston Bridge was built across Lake Guntersville, the largest lake in Alabama, in 1930 and was one of the original 15 Memorial Toll Bridges. The original George Houston Bridge was demolished in 1994 after receiving a failure inspection rating.

A Part of Guntersville, Alabama as viewed from Wyeth Rock

The George Houston Bridge may be seen in Background at Extreme Right   PHOTO BY J. O. FORRESTER

Residence Section, Looking Southeast from Square, Scottsboro, Ala.

Scottsboro was founded by Robert Scott, a North Carolina native who established many industries in the city. Scottsboro became famous in 1931 through the trial of the Scottsboro Boys, which drew international attention to the racial injustices of Alabama's legal system.

201

JACKSON COUNTY COURT HOUSE, SCOTTSBORO, ALA.

The Jackson County Courthouse was built in 1912 and is still in use. The trials of the Scottsboro Boys were held in this courthouse in 1931 and 1933. The courthouse was renovated in 1954 and new offices were added in 1967.

Built in 1893 by Frederick Aldhous, the Aldhous Block was a four-story stone and brick building that housed a bowling alley as well as the First National Bank. Aldhous Block was destroyed in a fire on January 23, 1937.

ALDHOUS BLOCK, BRIDGEPORT, ALA.

North Alabama was full of Liquor Interests, Big Mules, steel companies, Republicans, professors, and other persons of no background.

— HARPER LEE, *To Kill a Mockingbird*